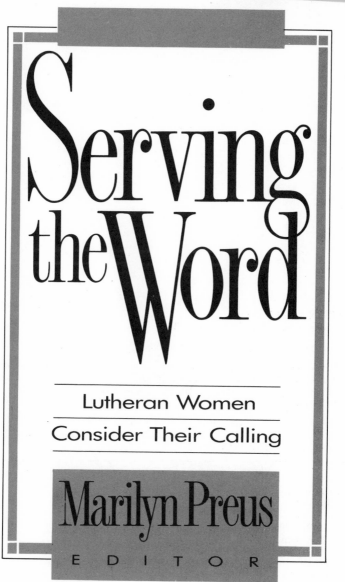

Serving the Word

Lutheran Women
Consider Their Calling

Marilyn Preus
EDITOR

AUGSBURG Publishing House • Minneapolis

SERVING THE WORD
Lutheran Women Consider Their Calling

Scripture quotations unless otherwise noted are from the Revised Standard Version of the Bible, copyright 1946, 1952, and 1971 by the Division of Christian Education of the National Council of Churches.

Library of Congress Cataloging-in-Publication Data

Serving the word: Lutheran women consider their calling/ Marilyn
    Preus, editor.
        p.   cm.
    ISBN 0-8066-2357-8
    1. Women in church work—Lutheran Church.   2. Women clergy.
3. Lutheran Church—Doctrines.   4. Evangelical Lutheran Church in
America—Doctrines.   5. Lutheran Church—Clergy.   6. Evangelical
Lutheran Church in America—Clergy.   I. Preus, Marilyn, 1932–
BX8074.W65S47   1988
262'.1441'088042—dc19   88-14537
                                                                          CIP

Manufactured in the U.S.A.   APH 10-5726

1   2   3   4   5   6   7   8   9   0   1   2   3   4   5   6   7   8   9

Contents

Dedication and Preface

This book is lovingly dedicated to the memory of Mabel Wold Sihler, a woman of this century, who served the Word in a variety of ways. While there are many notable Lutheran women whose stories could be told in a book about ministry, Mrs. Sihler's story is chosen because it is both representative and exemplary. Born of missionary parents in China, she grew up observing that Oriental culture, later becoming a missionary herself to the native Americans in Wisconsin. She was a teacher and a mother; and in the last years of her life, she became something of a prophet and a visionary, encouraging the church to accept an expanded view of women's vocation and ministry. The brief story of Mrs. Sihler's life which follows includes stories of other women whose lives are models of Christian commitment.

In February of 1979, four months before her death, Mabel Sihler gave three presentations to a gathering of women in North Dakota. A wonderful storyteller, she began by telling her own story and held the rapt attention of her audience for the next two days.

"I was born June 26, 1904, in Tzihor, Hupeh, China, to missionary parents, the fourth child in a family already blessed with three daughters. On my 16th birthday my father told this story:

'The night was steaming hot, hot and humid as a river town in central China can be at the end of June. Other missionaries had already fled the heat of the plains for the summer resort of

Bien Shan, but the Wolds had to wait for the imminent arrival of child number four. When labor began, our Chinese servant went out to broadcast the word that the baby was arriving. The business persons and officials of the town assembled in the mission courtyard, laden with gifts and strings of firecrackers. Patiently the throng waited as afternoon waned and the hot summer night descended (the birth was obviously a difficult and protracted one). Finally, as the first streaks of dawn lightened the horizon, the cook came out and said, (with a "nyaah,") "It's a girl." Into the mists of the morning the bearers of gifts and firecrackers vanished. Not *one* gift was left, not *one* firecracker was fired to celebrate the arrival into this world of Mabel Margrethe Wold, fourth daughter, rejected by the Chinese.'

"On July 2nd my mother was able to travel, so the family set out for the mountain resort to join the other missionaries already there, arriving on July 4th. Some of the missionary men, informed that the Wold family was en route up the mountain, ran down to meet them, and as the family came in sight, the men threw their hats in the air and shouted, 'Hurrah for the 4th!' My Dad concluded his story, 'I blushed because of the 4th.' And so it was, as a babe not 10 days old, I had been rejected by the Chinese, ridiculed by the whites, and an embarrassment to my father."

Years have passed, and still I hear the drama in her voice and the intensity of her passion as she spoke those three phrases. She traced her feminist consciousness back to the circumstances of her birth. And her good humor prevailed, as she continued:

"I didn't resent the story; I thought it was terribly funny. But the story does illustrate a worldwide attitude held in 1904 and in too many areas of the world in 1979: the value and importance attached to a male child and conversely the low value placed on the female. Had I been the fourth son, my father would have been blessed indeed, smiled upon by heaven. Great was the sympathy given him that he should be so unfortunate as to begat four daughters.

"Growing up in China, I was to learn firsthand how expendable females were. Girl babies in those days were often destroyed.

Girls were sold to the family of the husband-to-be at a very tender age. I saw how girl children suffered as the bones of their feet were broken and their feet bound into painful stumps on which they were able to walk only short distances. A widow often committed suicide at the grave of her husband because she knew her life as a widow would be a living hell. The plight of womanhood was indelibly set on my consciousness.

"Then I observed the women missionaries who seemed to go from pregnancy to pregnancy, from baby to baby. Some, like my mother, died at age 44. This isn't fair! A woman should have some protection from a cycle of one pregnancy after another; all through her child-bearing years, losing her figure, her teeth, her health, and finally her life. Is this what being a woman means? And if I don't marry I'm only half a person, an old maid.

"At a tender age I think I became a rebel. I could not understand how the church preached as dogma the bias of some of St. Paul's pronouncements and ignored the significance of Christ's treatment of women and his teachings.

"I came to the United States in 1922 to attend St. Olaf College. It was an exciting time to attend college. It was an exciting time to be a woman in America. In 1920, the 19th amendment had passed, giving women the vote. I could hardly wait for my 21st birthday so I could vote.

"At St. Olaf in that day professional counseling was totally unknown. The saying was that girls came to college to catch a husband; men to get an education and a profession. It was practically taken for granted that women would teach school until they got married; only men were encouraged to take administrative jobs. I resented and rebelled against the obvious pay discrimination between men and women teachers. So I read the biographies of women who had fought for women's rights: the rights to hold property, to have an education, to vote, and I learned at what cost those rights had been won. They were rights I could *never* take for granted."

Mrs. Sihler traced the history of women's struggle in America and concluded, "Someone had to organize all those parades, speeches, petitions, meetings, lobbying of legislators and congressmen. And in 1920 women got the vote. Think of the cost in woman power, self-denial, heartbreak, defeat, over and over, all the work they must do before they achieved the right that should have been theirs all along."

In a similar manner, she vividly recounted the struggle for passage of the Equal Rights Amendment, proposed in 1923 by Alice Paul, and still a subject for debate in state legislatures. "Why have I taken the time to recount this history? Does it have anything to do with my responsibility to the church? I would say it definitely does. I am a woman. I am a citizen. I enjoy rights and privileges that other women have won for me. I am a Christian woman. For the way that I use my rights and privileges, I am accountable. What happens on the political and social scene is reflected in the church."

As an example, Mrs. Sihler told of the beginnings of church women's organizations. When three churches merged in 1917 and the Norwegian Lutheran Church was formed, a Women's Missionary Federation (WMF) was organized. Lena Dahl became the first president. "Mrs. Dahl had already banded women of the United Synod for cooperative effort and had led them for six years. [As president of that earlier WMF organization], she had long been distressed by the poor homes missionaries had to come to when home on furlough. 'Could we do something to make their stay in America more pleasant and more comfortable?' she wondered. Thoughts were a prelude to prayer and action for Mrs. Dahl. One year later in 1913, at a Federation meeting, ground was broken for two missionary cottages on a hill back of the seminary. They were the first of their kind. They stood as a unique piece of missionary work and a memorial to Lena Dahl's zeal and devotion."

Lena Dahl is one of several women mentioned in *Serving the Word* who had the vision and commitment to organize in order to do the work of the kingdom at home and in foreign lands. It is almost impossible to think of what the church would have been, down through the years, without the witness and service of women. But the work of our mothers and grandmothers was not always valued and appreciated. Mabel Sihler goes on to talk about that:

". . . the first years were difficult and discouraging for the women of this new organization as the clergy, especially, criticized their efforts, 'So now the women are going to take over the church! Hasn't Paul explicitly said _____?'

"Women in leadership have commonly heard remarks like, 'You can see who wears the pants in that family,' and 'Why doesn't she stay home where she belongs and take care of her husband and children?' It took determination and a lot of starch for our church women in a work that raised their sights and stimulated their spiritual growth.

"Not only did they provide houses fully furnished to accommodate missionaries home on furlough, they supported a variety of missionary projects: a school for girls, a school and mission for Indians in America, missionary work in Africa, a worker in Alaska. The Women's Missionary Federation of the American Lutheran Church (merged in 1931) supported missions in India and later in New Guinea.

"The women felt a need for Bible study at their meetings. Such studies, they were told, should be written and conducted by men. Women were not qualified. So the first WMF Bible studies were written by theological professors and taught by clergy. Even some of the circuit conventions were conducted by the pastor of the local church.

"For all this growth of the women's organization in the church, no one had ever challenged the system which is patriarchal. The Bible was written by men, translated by men, interpreted by men. The church was organized by men, all decisions as to polity and doctrine were developed and implemented by men. As more educated women entered the ranks of leadership in the WMF and the ALC women's organization, they began to write their own Bible studies and conduct their own conventions. They turned over large sums of money to the synodical budget for mission work and other specified programs and somehow the men found this was perfectly OK; it really helped the work of the church.

The women also determined where other sums of money were to be spent and they began to question the male hierarchy.

"This is our church too. We comprise over 50% of the membership. We provide the support systems of the church, but we have no representation in the decision-making bodies of the church.

"And women and men began to question some of the theological assumptions on which men based their authority."

Mrs. Sihler had given a vivid historical account of women's struggle for equality and liberation, and now she probed the Scripture and somewhat breathlessly told the beginning of early church structures, showing the effects. "As in secular government, so in the church, women had no vote, no representation on boards or committees; but the women of the church banded together for support of missions and for Bible study and prayer. Their numbers grew until every circuit and every district was organized under the national Missionary Federation. I remember a circuit convention in rural Wisconsin (I was president at the time). The ushers came to me and said, 'Well, Mrs. Sihler, are you satisfied? Every seat is taken. Chairs down the aisle are full. Women are even sitting around the communion rail. Shall we hang them from the chandeliers?' Attendance at conventions was tremendous. Women became a great force."

In the second presentation, Mrs. Sihler recited stories from the life of Jesus which illustrate his attitude toward women. "I believe that Christ has given us, in the Gospels, an appreciation of our value in his eyes, not previously emphasized in Sunday school and confirmation instruction and in Bible studies. Because of the stirrings within the church among men and women regarding the stereotyping of the sexes and traditional roles, in the late 1960s, the Division of Theological Studies of the Lutheran Council in the U.S.A. established a study on the ordination of women. . . . After two years of study the commission could find no conclusive argument either for or against the ordination of women so it was left up to the Lutheran synods themselves to decide the issue."

With unrelenting energy and a feisty good humor, Mrs. Sihler traced developments in the American Lutheran Church, challenging opinions with which she did not agree. All this she knew well, having been the chairperson of the Task Force on Full Participation of Women in the Church which was authorized by the 1974 convention of the American Lutheran Church. It had two purposes: to monitor progress toward implementation of guidelines contained in the statement adopted in 1972, "Women and Men in Church and Society—Toward Wholeness in the Christian Community," and to make recommendations to the national Church Council on subjects such as women clergy, the changing roles of pastors and mates in congregational ministry, the vocational potential of women in professional church service, church employment policies, increased frequency of divorce in American society, and sexist language in ALC communication vehicles.

"Did the task force accomplish anything?" she asked in her talk at the North Dakota retreat. "I think it did. For example, as a result of the work of the task force, today we have guidelines for avoiding bias in the publications of the American Lutheran Church. We did a monumental review of all curriculum, publications, brochures, programs; we documented sexism in language, stereotyping in pictures and programs; and we recommended the adoption of guidelines for all facets of church communication and printed material. The new hymnbook (*Lutheran Book of Worship*, 1978) reflects this awareness. I worked so long on all of that material that I almost hate to go down to the church headquarters now because people tell me, 'Mabel, when you come around, we all get nervous.'

"We designed a questionnaire to learn the variety and extent of the participation of women in the corporate life of the congregation. We made a survey of women's positions in the national church offices and on district staffs and learned that women are rarely in leadership roles and most often on support staff. Our research has reinforced the equal rights and equal opportunity statements which the church has adopted."

Mabel was well qualified to lead a task force on the participation of women in the church. Her whole life, from her birth in China through the first 70 years of this century, had prepared her for this. She reflected back on her experiences and applied them to the assignment.

She was the daughter of talented parents. Her father was the first president of the Lutheran Church of China and the Lutheran Theological Seminary. He was a teacher and evangelist as well as a Chinese scholar who translated Chinese novels into English. Mabel said of her mother, "My mother was every bit as much a missionary as my father. She was a qualified teacher and taught Chinese girls in the mission schools." Their unusual experiences as missionaries in China were recalled by Mabel for the Oral History and Archives Collection of the Midwest China Center in St. Paul, Minn. In this reminiscence she tells many wonderful stories. One tale of how her mother maintained family traditions even under the most adverse circumstances is fascinating.

A few days before Christmas 1911, with rumors of war circulating, the missionaries and their families evacuated the interior and were put on river junks bound for Hankow. The children wondered what kind of Christmas they would have in this setting. But the parents were very resourceful. A grocery box covered with red crepe paper and studded with lighted candles became their Christmas tree. Mabel's "Mama" produced the traditional Norwegian feast: lutefisk (which she had made from dried cod soaked in lye), lefse, and all the fancy Christmas goodies they had had at home. "How she ever did it, I don't know. But Mama was a genius and the cooks were cooperative, so we had our regular Christmas feast supper." After devotions in Chinese and English and the opening of gifts, they joined missionaries from other boats in singing Christmas carols.

After Mabel's mother died, Pastor Wold married Anna Lee, a capable and dedicated woman who left her mark on the family. Mabel wrote to me following our time together at the retreat:

"Right now I'm over my eyebrows in my stepmother's letters. Mother Wold was a single missionary in China from 1904–1920 when she married my father. He died in October 1928 and Mother went back into the work as a single again. In 1932, when she was home on furlough, the church informed her they could not afford to send her back to China. Convinced that her call was from the Lord, she signed an agreement with the synod that they had no responsibility for her, only that she be permitted to work on our field out there. When she had enough money, through the gifts of friends, to buy a ticket to China, she went and was supported by faith for a year out there when the Mission asked her to go on salary. She worked until 1940 and in 1941, when she planned to return, the Japanese attacked Pearl Harbor. But in 1946 she again returned to China. She was then 69 and the church would *not* send her, but she found the money and went. As I read her letters and the amazing fruits of her labors out there, I am struck again and again with the remarkable courage, faith, vision, and vigor as well as the imagination and leadership she evinced."

Mabel Wold was married for 36 years to Pastor Ernest Sihler. After serving a Lutheran congregation in Minnesota, they became missionaries to the Winnebago and Oneida Indians at Bethany Indian Mission in Wittenberg, Wisconsin. During their 20 years in Wisconsin, Mrs. Sihler was editor of *Christian Home*, a publication of the Homme Children's Home.

[One cannot mention the Homme Home in a book about women in ministry without recalling Ingeborg Swenholt Homme, 1845–1926, wife of pioneer Pastor E. J. Homme. "The story of Pastor Homme's life reads almost like a fairy tale . . . he founded the town of Wittenberg and got a train to connect with it. Then he built a parsonage, an orphanage, an old people's home, a printing plant, a saw mill, an academy, a normal school, an Indian mission, a church, and a new orphanage" (*Some Marthas and Marys of the NLCA: Life Sketches of Pioneer Lutheran Women First in Their Field*, Augsburg).

But all this not without the help of Mrs. Homme, whose inheritance and endurance helped to enable the projects to succeed. In an article which appeared in "For Gammel og Ung" (For Old and Young), a paper Pastor Homme published, it is said, "Mrs.

Homme's greatness consisted in her perfect character as a good woman, in her pure, noble, and self-sacrificing mind and faithfulness."

The area around Wittenberg was a wilderness at the time the Hommes settled there. Mrs. Homme was often left to manage alone when her husband was away. She was not only a mother to her own eight children, but to the children who came to the orphanage as well. When help was needed in the old people's home and when the German Academy burned and students were left homeless, Mrs. Homme stepped in to help.

Her life, like the lives of so many women, though requiring more sacrifice and bravery than moderns can imagine, is only slenderly recorded in history. When there are accomplishments that can be measured, in one way or another, these people make it into history books; but lives marked by enduring loyalty and daily nurturing in love are often overlooked. Mrs. Homme calls those to mind.]

Mabel Sihler brought some of the same gracious hospitality and helpfulness to the Sihlers' ministry, qualities that are difficult to measure and acknowledge. But she was living in quite a different Wittenberg than the one Ingeborg Homme knew. Other opportunities were open to her. She became the first woman elected to the public school Board of Education and the first woman to serve as board president.

The Sihlers moved to Minneapolis in 1955 and Mabel served on the staff of the parish education department of the former Evangelical Lutheran Church and later managed the films department of Augsburg Publishing House from 1958 until her retirement in 1973.

As a result of her work with the Task Force on the Full Participation of Women in the Church, she served with a continuing Committee on Women's Concerns and gave speeches throughout the country. She was scheduled to give the keynote address at the National Youth Gathering in Kansas City, Mo. in August 1979 and to go to China in the fall. When she was with us in North Dakota in February she told us about the China trip. In her thank-you note she wrote me: "I had a phone call from a

Chinese professor. He knows two of the places I want to go to and is sure I'll get there but it may take longer than October to arrange the trip." But these plans did not materialize. Death intervened.

She became ill while visiting one of her three daughters and died less than a month later on Pentecost Sunday, June 3, 1979. The annual Mabel Sihler Lecture Series at Luther College, Decorah, Iowa, honors the memory of this gracious and talented woman of faith.

MARILYN PREUS

Introduction

This book is written with several audiences in mind. I think first of the students in a seminary class I teach called "Women in Ministry." As we have talked about the service and ministry of women from several different angles (biblical, historical, and sociological), I have been grateful for the books written by Reformed and Catholic scholars and writers. But because I am working with Lutheran students, preparing for a variety of service in the church and in the world, it is important that our conversations reflect our own confessional heritage and the service of women in this tradition. That makes a book like this necessary. While it does not do justice to *all* aspects of women's involvement in the church, this book makes a beginning, and is only one of many that should be written.

These essays are written by people from the three Lutheran churches (The American Lutheran Church [ALC], The Lutheran Church in America [LCA], and The Association of Evangelical Lutheran Churches [AELC]) which merged to form the Evangelical Lutheran Church in America (ELCA). The book is intended, as well, for a much broader community. The writers' stories and observations which celebrate life fully lived, are the stories of many readers whose ministry is characterized by devotion and commitment.

In one way and another, the writers explore the baptismal call to discipleship, the relationship and roles of clergy and laity, the call of some to the ministry of Word and Sacrament, and the Lutheran understanding of *ministry* and how it relates to *vocation* and *service*. One hopes that these reflections will contribute to the ongoing study of ministry in the Evangelical Lutheran Church in America.

This book is not meant to be limited to an "interior" conversation, but makes clear that Lutheran women have a great deal to contribute to ecumenical discussions, especially as concerns the subject of ministry. Our personal histories and theological work are noticeably absent from any of the current collections of thought having to do with women in the church and that makes the need for this book all the more obvious. One would hope that people of other churches will read our stories as eagerly as we have read theirs.

"Serving the Word" is one way of stating a phrase Martin Luther used often in his writings. In his treatise *Concerning the Ministry* (1523), Luther wrote, "A Christian is born to the Ministry of the Word in Baptism. . . the church is nothing without the Word and everything in it exists by virtue of the Word alone. . . . *the ministry of the Word belongs to all*" (*Luther's Works*, 40, 4ff.) (emphasis mine). Here, as elsewhere, Luther shows that "serving the gospel" is the duty upon which everything else depends and is common to all Christians. The chapters of this book give examples of some of the ways in which Lutheran women have understood their call to "serve the Word."

To set the tone for chapters that follow, *Gracia Grindal* reviews dominant themes in Lutheran doctrine and practice and shows how our confessional tradition shapes our understanding of the service and ministry of women. Though the documents of the Reformation have not been radical in their understanding of women, neither have they denied their humanity and full participation in the church.

This chapter, as others, refers to Articles V and VII of the *Augsburg Confession*. These articles have shaped the understanding Lutherans have about the church and its ministry. The *Confession*, a statement made in Augsburg in 1530 for the purpose of stating the Lutheran case to the pope and emperors, has been considered to be an important declaration of faith from the first. It has served as an ecumenical document which begins conversations for Lutherans, and speaks of what is necessary, not what is desirable.

Historian *L. DeAne Lagerquist* critiques particular ways of looking at the church that eliminate women from its history. She
suggests four biblical images (hospitality, patronage, teaching,
and administration) which provide a way of recovering the service
of women in the household of God. She asks: Are these four gifts
of the Spirit, expressed in the service of women, valued and
encouraged? What is the relationship between the past and present service of women?

Mary Hull Mohr provides an answer to the second question as
she reflects on the private/public service of women in the church
by thinking of her own vocation as a college professor in light of
her mother's life and service as a pastor's wife. She looks ahead
to the church of the future and treasures those gifts and goals
continuous in women's service that build community and create
a "home" in the church and in the world.

Anne Kanten speaks on behalf of the large segment of the
church that is rural and challenges women to be politically active
in protecting the special province given us by our Creator, the
care and stewardship of life and land.

Deaconess *E. Louise Williams* traces the scriptural basis for the
diaconate, gives a brief historical overview, and thinks about the
future by asking the question, "Now that women can be ordained, is there a need for the diaconate?"

In her experience as a volunteer trainer, *Marlene Wilson* has
observed that the church has not effectively used nor fully appreciated the service of volunteers. Combining social analysis
with Lutheran theology, she suggests that renewal in the church
would mean a new understanding of authentic discipleship and
a celebration of the role volunteers play in bringing that about.

Is it helpful to separate church people into two groups, "lay"
and "ordained"? How do we speak of the ministry of each? If
in some ways these questions have been intensified by the ordination of women, at least we have had to think about them in
new ways. *Eva Rogness* struggles with these questions, and others, showing how our language reflects or misrepresents our theology, and how the whole matter gets us into all sorts of problems.

Her chapter introduces several chapters in which ordained women, called to the ministry of Word and Sacrament are heard on a variety of subjects which affect them particularly.

Arguments for and against ordination have been made from Scripture, tradition, nature, and the masculine and feminine in God; but most people involved in this discussion turn to the Bible as the final authority. *Janet Landwehr* explores several of the texts relevant to the subject, while pointing out that the gospel empowers us all to wholeness.

Other writers reflect on their own personal experience as they think about what it means to be ordained. How is a person "called" to the ministry of Word and Sacrament? *Jane Strohl* clarifies the ways in which the call of God is mediated through the community, the church. *Stephanie Frey* describes her experience as worship leader and preacher and speculates on the response of congregations to the voice of women proclaiming the creative and redeeming Word. *Norene Smith* and *Paul Overvold* invite the reader into their shared private and professional lives as a clergy couple. They speak frankly about the flexibility and cooperation required to be faithful to their calls and model mutuality in both marriage and ministry. *Ruth Drews'* assignment was to write about the authority of the office of the ministry. She begins by describing the state of her office, her study, which is only slightly less chaotic than the urban setting in which she is daily challenged to do authentic ministry. *Constance Parvey* writes a symbolic essay on the subject of space that is really about power. (It makes one think of Katakshamma Paul Raj, from India, who said that when she was a little girl she sensed the low status of females and tried not to take up too much space, or breathe too much air, but made herself as small as possible.) Ordained women, Parvey says, discover how to fill a space they have never filled before. The chapter concludes with a wonderful ending on a strong Lutheran theme.

The book has intentionally used familiar images from the traditional experience of women: serving, household, hospitality. The concluding chapter is about ecumenism, a word that means household, or family living in one house. *Carol Birkland* points out the need for everyone in the family to have a voice in what goes on there and for all to let the Holy Spirit have its way in bringing about unity.

Women have been serving the Word for centuries, ever since the days when women traveled with Jesus and the disciples and "provided for them out of their means" (Luke 8:1-3). Mary Magdalene is mentioned in that group. In all four Gospels she is seen at the cross and at the tomb. And on Easter morning when Jesus appeared to her, and said, "Go and tell," she went to proclaim the resurrection to Jesus' followers (John 20). The early church called her "the apostle to the apostles."

It is a great loss to the church that her witness has been suppressed. She had been healed by Jesus and she became a faithful, loving follower, obedient to his final commission. By her presence in the Christian history that we claim, she enriches our understanding of what it means to serve the Word.

MARILYN PREUS

Feast of Mary Magdalene, July 22

1

Women in Lutheran Tradition

GRACIA GRINDAL

When I was growing up in a Lutheran Free Church parsonage in the '50s, I knew that our small, radical church body had a clear doctrine of the ministry: All Christians were servants, and the pastor was the servant of the congregation, the one who assured that the gospel was being rightly preached and the sacraments rightly administered. Any behavior by the pastor which indicated he was above the people was met with cruel scorn. Lutheran pastors from other Lutheran traditions, I observed, did not act like servants. They seemed to be more what tradition calls *Herr Pastor*. Their credentials were as impeccably Lutheran as my father's. What was the difference? Was there a Lutheran understanding of ministry? Is there one today that prevails throughout the Lutheran churches? What has happened to this doctrine now that women are being ordained in many Lutheran churches? Something has changed. Now, after more than 15 years of ordaining women, we are beginning to understand what a major development it has been for the churches and how it has forced us back into biblical texts, Lutheran doctrine, and our various American Lutheran traditions.

It is generally agreed that Martin Luther, whose reformation of medieval theology set off movements and ideas which have still not run their course, is one of the most creative intellects in Western thought. He never ceases to surprise those searching his writings for theological insight. One who looks in the indices of Luther's voluminous works to discover his attitudes toward women can find practically anything. Luther was a man of his time: an Augustinian monk, heir to over 2000 years of Western misogyny (hatred towards women). To expect that he would champion the liberation of women is too much. At the same time, Luther was surprisingly critical of misogyny and made insightful comments about the church which expected its leaders to shun marriage and women in order to serve God.

For our purposes, a more fruitful study of Luther comes from examining the crucial doctrines he developed and judging them for their relevance to women as well as men. That might help us see how Luther unleashed a revolution far broader than he could have imagined, ideas which today can, perhaps, make it possible for women to achieve full participation in the life and ministry of the church.

Luther's fundamental belief was that the only righteousness which can save humanity is what he called the "alien righteousness" of Christ. This doctrine, popularly known as justification by faith, turned out to be a frontal attack on the medieval church which had developed an elaborate system of penance and merits. By Luther's time, ordinary Christians could buy indulgences from the church for the remission of the temporal punishment of their sins. The theory was that the saints, through their good works, had built up a treasury of merits which could be transferred to those who needed some to shorten their time in purgatory, and hasten the soul's journey to paradise. It was the selling of indulgences which so outraged Luther that he nailed the 95 Theses to the door of Wittenberg church. A sinner, Luther thundered, only dared to stand before a righteous God clothed in the righteousness of Christ. All other righteousness, even that of the most holy saint, was as filthy rags to God.

Luther pressed the doctrine of justification against all the structures of the church. As a result of this theological insight, he urged the doctrine of the priesthood of all believers as the biblically correct way to understand one's life as a Christian. All Christians were priests, freed by God's gift of salvation in Christ, to *minister* to each other for their mutual consolation and edification.

It seems obvious that such a doctrine would pose serious problems for the medieval church. Luther disapproved of celibacy as a requirement for the clergy because, among other things, it set the priest apart from most believers. Luther could find no warrant for such a doctrine in the Bible. Priests could claim no special *charism* (gift): ordination did not confer a new, more holy character on the priest as the church said. In fact, Luther found little, if anything, in the Bible about ordination. *All* Christians were priests. For Luther, the ordained minister's chief role in the community was to proclaim the Word. For this reason they needed to be educated to assure the congregation that the gospel was being purely preached and the sacraments rightly administered. Those code words in Lutheran language mean that pastors had to be theologically trained to distinguish between the law and gospel in order to guard the gospel. Law, according to Luther in the Heidelberg Disputation, is that which accurately diagnoses the human condition, as in a medical diagnosis, so that people will know they need healing from the Great Physician.

It is important to note how radically Luther's theology pared down the medieval idea of what was necessary for ministry. Article VII of the *Augsburg Confession,* the document which Lutherans look to for guidance, states that

> . . . it is sufficient for the true unity of the Christian church that the Gospel be preached in conformity with a pure understanding of it and that the sacraments be administered in accordance with the divine Word.

There is nothing in the article about what kind of a person the preacher or celebrant should be. One knowing the history of the argument on ministry in the church can hear in the language of the article an implicit attack on what has come to be called the threefold ministry, or the historic episcopate. By Luther's time, the church taught that the bishop was the sign of the visible unity of the churches, and that where the bishop was, there was the church. Neither Article V or VII deny this explicitly. They simply state that it is enough that there be Word and Sacrament. One can, of course, imagine that quite a bit depends on how the gospel is defined. For Lutherans it is in the Word and Sacrament. So Lutherans can see the gospel in Catholic Word and Sacrament; the Roman hierarchy does not, quite, see the gospel in Lutheran Word and Sacrament because, as the U.S. Bishops Committee on Doctrine wrote in its response to the Lutheran–Catholic Dialogue VII: Justification by Faith, "apostolic succession in office (through the sacrament of episcopal ordination) is not simply important for the transmission of the deposit of faith, but necessary" (*Lutheran Quarterly* NS1, 1987). That is the crux of the theological disagreement; it continues to this day as the chief stumbling block to ecumenical accord. In addition, Catholic thought (and the most recent statements of Pope John Paul II reaffirm this) is deeply committed to the theology of resemblance: the priest must resemble Christ, as well as represent him. This means that the priest must be male.

To sum up Luther's doctrine of the ministry—more correctly the doctrine of the Word—would be to say that all ministry is under the Word. Luther thought of all believers as servants of the Word. Pastors had a special responsibility to the Word, to see that it was rightly preached and the sacraments rightly administered. No matter how the church was organized, congregationally or episcopally, the Word was what called the church into being, the Word was what pastors were called to serve. Thus, when Lutherans looked in the *Augsburg Confession* to see what barriers there were to ordaining women, there were none. The main obstacles were the Pauline injunctions against women speaking in church, and the ecumenical problem which would be posed by this action, especially where our ecumenical partners do not and will not ordain women. For Lutherans, structural organization has always been *adiaphoron*, a matter of indifference deserving local and contemporary theological argument and thought. Now that women are being ordained in the Lutheran church and not in the Catholic church, that may be changing. If one can prove that a certain form of ecclesiastical structure is inimical to the ordination of women, should Lutherans avoid those structures or give up the ordination of women because it is a matter of *adiaphoron* which is keeping us from unity?

Luther's reworking of the doctrine of the Word also had a great effect on the laity and their self-understanding. Most radical was his new thought concerning vocation in the Christian life. The medieval church had understood vocation to be purely religious: one *made* a vocation by leaving the world and becoming a monk or nun. Luther took that commonly held assumption and recast it.

It may be helpful to draw some distinctions at this point: the priesthood of all believers is generally understood to be the *ministry* of Christians, under the gospel. Then, having been freed by the Word, we are immediately called to work. That is *vocation*. It is not a priestly work; it is our life with others, our work, our social obligations—what we were physically created for. When Christians respond to the needs of the neighbor, no matter how menial a task it is, they reflect this attitude described by Luther:

> O God, because I am certain that thou hast created me as a man and hast from my body begotten this child, I also know for a certainty that it meets with thy perfect pleasure. I confess to thee that I am not worthy to rock the little babe or wash its diapers, or to be entrusted with the care of the child and its mother. How is it that I, without any merit, have come to this distinction of being certain that I am serving thy creature and thy most precious will? O how gladly I will do so, though the duties should be even more insignificant and despised. Neither frost nor heat, neither drudgery nor labor, will distress or dissuade me, for I am certain that it is thus pleasing in thy sight. (*Luther's Works*, vol. 45, pp. 39-40)

We each play several different roles in society; these are all part of our vocation. One of the ways God sustains creation is through our faithful work in these different roles. For example,

God gives human beings strong sexual drives so that they are drawn together. Though we pervert and misuse this powerful gift, marriage and family are still God's gift to us. In the same way, work is both gift and curse. Sin changed the delights Adam and Eve had in their work, but, in Christian faith, work can once again be pursued joyfully, to the glory of God. Likewise, citizenship, the political sphere, shunned as evil by many, is also a duty and delight.

Luther thought of vocation as being deeply rooted in Baptism. In our Baptism, a daily dying and rising in Christ, the old nature struggles against the new to live. Our old nature is bound to boast when it does good for a neighbor; in Christ we are dead to such boasting, even though we may suffer for our good deed. As Luther says in his essay on Baptism, the reason death is so painful is that sin hates to die. Both men and women have been baptized; Christ is born in each of them, equally. Both have sin in them which must be put to death by the gracious act of God in Christ Jesus. Both men and women were equally culpable because their sin was unbelief, not pride.

It is precisely here that we can begin to see the impact of Luther's theology on women. If Baptism is the sacrament which radically changes people, and frees them for both the priesthood of all believers and their vocations in the world, then women are included in a way they had not been before. No Christian has a ministry superior to another; no vocation is more Christian than another. Now, instead of being the gateway to hell, as a good many Christian theologians called them in the early church, women can now be members of the royal priesthood and persons of importance to the community. This should have been, and apparently was for some women, an invitation to equality in the church's life and mission.

As with all revolutions, the Reformation may have promised more than it could deliver to women. Feminists have noted that the loss of the convents did impoverish the sophisticated culture of women who, at least inside the walls, were able to control their own destinies. Being removed from that life into a marriage in which they might suffer abuse and the frequent perils of child-birth may not have been a net gain for every woman. Mary Potter Engel of United Theological Seminary in New Brighton, Minnesota (and previously at Luther Northwestern Theological Seminary), argues persuasively that both Luther and Calvin asserted the equality of women in the spiritual estate, while keeping them submissive in the everyday world.

Be that as it may, Luther was the first major theologian in the West since before Augustine, who did not think that the love of God and love of woman were contradictory drives. Single women, mothers, and wives could take courage from their new sense of vocation as members of family, workers, and citizens. Luther's theology of creation and thus marriage and family made him an implacable foe of celibacy. This had a dramatic effect on both the theology of ministry and the institutions which acted out that theology: the monasteries and convents in Germany. As these institutions of long standing in the community emptied out, monks and nuns married, with Luther's hearty approval. He even surprised himself by marrying Katherine von Bora. Though the evidence is that he could be a cranky and demanding spouse, he loved his wife, delighting in her skill at managing him and the fairly substantial estate she built up over the years. It means something that Luther, a conservative man, went against custom by willing her the property so she would not be beholden to the eldest son, as was the custom in Luther's time. It is also important to note that Luther did urge the education of women when it was a very new idea.

There is some evidence as well, that women, especially the wives or daughters of the reformers, were taken with Luther's theology. Sexist as the Renaissance was, it was a genuine revival of learning. So it is not surprising to discover that unusual women did obtain learning. Olympia Morata, an Italian Lutheran woman, was appointed to teach Greek at the University of Heidelberg, but illness prevented her from doing so. Other women, like Margreta Blarer (1494–1541), chose to remain celibate, something Luther had approved of when the person had a gift for it, in order to work as deaconesses in the community. Martin Bucer, a colleague of Luther's, thought Blarer's work so insightful that he corresponded frequently with her in Latin. These exceptions, though they are worth pondering, do not disprove Mary Potter Engel's thesis.

■ ■ ■

Though it is too broad a leap, it is not really until the 19th century that we see much development in the vocations of either women or men outside of the home. With the coming of the Industrial Revolution, a new kind of family emerged. In this model the man left the home to work at a job which seemed radically disjunctive with the care and nurture of the family, while the woman was left at home to take over all of the tasks of care and nurture. Women gained control of the private, moral, emotionally secure, religious world which rarely intersected with the male world of industry and control. This made it easy to redefine Christian vocation along sexist lines: a man's vocation was his career, a woman's, her family. It is a disappointment to see how easily that happened, but not difficult. Father's care for the family is shown by his dedication to earning money to support the family; mother's career is the actual labor required to nurture and care for the family's physical needs. Luther was very careful not to divide things up in that way: both mother and father were entrusted with the care of the child, from changing diapers to caring for the other spouse.

It is precisely out of this world that the women's movement began. During the 19th century, women began meeting together in church groups for mutual support and consolation: the priesthood of all believers. It is pretty much agreed that the response of women to the needs of women in non-Christian lands was the beginning of the feminist movement in both England and America. Lutheran women in this country were too busy settling the frontiers to follow suit immediately. But after the Civil War, thousands of Lutheran "Ladies' Aids" began. These organizations gave women a place to share in the ministries of the church.

By the end of the century, Lutheran men and women were supporting deaconesses with important, though traditional, roles in the congregation and community. They were listening to women missionaries speak to them about their work in foreign lands. They must have noted, as well, that local "Ladies' Aids" were forming national organizations with considerable skills at raising money to support a wide variety of mission enterprises throughout the world. One can say, without too much fear of exaggeration, that it was women missionaries, empowered by these groups, who functioned as the first women to serve as pastors in the Lutheran tradition. Most Lutherans remember that these women were the first women preachers they had ever heard and in their stories of the mission field we learned that they preached the Word, cast out demons, baptized infants in emergencies, and prophesied, things they could have done at home only with some difficulty.

At the same time, women were entering the arena of education. None of the rather impressive colleges built by Lutherans in this country would be what it is today without the dedicated leadership of the first and second generation of women teachers who gave much so that the institutions could live. The list deserves better treatment elsewhere, but who of us can deny their effect on thousands of future pastors, pastor's wives, missionaries, teachers, nurses, and countless others who fulfilled their Christian vocations outside of church employment, but who brought to their work the values imparted by these women.

When I began teaching at Luther College in 1968, I was fully aware of my place in that tradition of women whose professional commitment to the church gave them something of a public ministry. Working for the church, however, was not to be understood as a vocation superior to working for any other secular organization. Christian vocation had been preached to me in the language of service. I felt no sense whatever that the ordained ministry was superior to that of education, law, or medicine. My heroes in the faith (many of them strong and dedicated women like Gerda Mortensen, the long time Dean of Women at Augsburg College) had given me every reason to think one could be a woman

and run a church and college with every bit as much authority
as a man. The best preacher at Augsburg, President B. M. Chris-
tensen, was adamant, as his predecessors the Sverdrups had been,
that ordination was not necessary to their vocation as seminary
presidents. The idea of Christian vocation as service was burned
into me by these people. But vocation was not ministry; it was
service in the world—God, hidden like yeast in the loaf, working
to sustain creation.

By 1970, I was aware that there was an argument going on
about the ordination of women. I, like everyone else, came to
the conversation out of my background. A woman pastor would
be a servant of the Word. The few articles which treated the issue
in the church press argued almost exclusively from Scripture,
with some few references to *The Book of Concord*, or Luther's
writings, that women should or should not be ordained. The
study booklet, *The Ordination of Women*, condensed from the
study documents of the American Lutheran Church (ALC) and
Lutheran Church in America (LCA) by Raymond Tiemeyer in
1970, dealt mainly with the difficult biblical texts. In the specific
chapter on how the Lutheran tradition thought of women, there
is a preponderance of references to comments on how Luther or
his contemporaries viewed women, since there was nothing in
the *Augsburg Confession* which either included or excluded them
as pastors. When the Luther Seminary faculty, pressed by the
ALC Church Council to review four objections to the ordination
of women—biblical, theological, practical and ecumenical—they
found only the ecumenical objection serious enough to consider.
They concluded that the matter was "difficult to assess" (*The
Ordination of Women*, Augsburg, 1970, p. 36). Their foresight
proved to be clear: today women pastors are a source of great
difficulty in ecumenical conversations between churches who do
ordain women and those who do not.

When the conventions of the ALC and the LCA voted in 1970
to approve the ordination of women, few of us knew what an
upheaval would occur in our own lives, or in the life of the church.
That it made everyone rethink what it meant to be ordained as
a Lutheran goes without saying. What it means to have a woman

pastor has not yet been posed to every member of the Evangelical Lutheran Church in America (ELCA): it is still possible for call committees to avoid women candidates, though that grows more difficult with time. One can be sure that each tradition informs how Lutherans think of women pastors. The women clergy shaped by the tradition of the *Herr Pastor* enter the clergy roster with the idea that they take on considerable authority with their stole. I am proud to say that the congregations rooted in my tradition were among the quickest to call women pastors; as one might expect, they could also be most wicked if the woman pastor got uppity, or for some reason did not work out.

There are some general things one can say about the ordination of women and the new thinking their presence requires. For one, the relation of the woman pastor to the women's organization was a new thing. How did the woman pastor maintain her loyalty to women and the women's organization while also serving, or at least, wanting to serve the entire congregation? Was the woman pastor the pastor only to the women? Was she in fact a part of the women's organization and obligated to bring jello salads to the "Ladies' Aid"?

A corollary of that was what happened to the pastor's wife. She had long been considered like a pastor to the women's organization. Though that system was in decline by 1970, it was still robust enough to cause some uneasy moments for male pastors, pastors' wives, and female pastors. The role of the pastor's husband is an emerging one which is just now developing. What those men will have to say about their roles in the church should be interesting as well.

Another question that women pastors posed was what it meant to be laity. Women had always been laity. Now the role of the laity was called into question. It is not surprising that at this time the laity became increasingly worried about their place in the church. At the same time the liturgical movement was sweeping through the churches with its stress on lay participation in the liturgy. Some interpreted the priesthood of all believers to mean the clericalization of the laity: by putting on albs and standing up in front of the church, both lay men and women could achieve stature in the church because they were doing what the clergy had done. For Luther this would have been an alarming development. It was exactly the theology he had opposed so vigorously. Luther had demolished the idea that it takes more authority to consecrate the sacrament than to proclaim the Word in several of his treatises, among them *The Babylonian Captivity of the Church*. With the rise of the laity in the churches, lay men and women were preaching, but not celebrating the Sacrament. To some it looked as though we were right back where we started. By an odd course of events, we seemed to be back to a theology of ordination which made it a special *charism* necessary for a valid sacrament.

The ordination of women caused, in turn, a loss of identity among the male clergy. Just what did it mean to be clergy now that women could be clergy and any lay person could preach? It should not be surprising that the ALC, and then later the LCA began to favor the title *bishop* to assure that their district presidents would be accorded the same dignity and pride of place as Catholic or Methodist bishops. The title may have seemed innocent enough, but words have histories. As soon as the title was well in place, the scholars and bishops themselves began studying what exactly bishops did in the New Testament and early Christian church.

What they found was the Catholic doctrine of the ministry, the very doctrine which Luther had attacked so vigorously. The ironies are rich. The ordination of women (made possible by Luther's doctrine that the minister was a servant of, not a visible stand-in for Christ) was so unsettling to the structures that the very doctrine of the historic episcopate which had for centuries excluded women was the one to which Lutheran theologians, pastors, and bishops were increasingly attracted, no matter what their particular tradition of ordained ministry.

As a teacher of preaching at a Lutheran seminary, I believe, as the leaders of my particular branch of Lutheranism, and Luther, taught, that all Christians have the ministry of the Word and do proclaim the Word to each other in their daily ministries as Christians. If they want to become full-time pastors, they should go to the seminary to train for the calling which will entrust them with the gospel. Now that women can be ordained, they have one more vocation in the church open to them. If they want to preach and care for souls, there is a place for them to study and await the call of the church. But I hope that the Lutheran church will continue to encourage the variety of vocations it now offers to both men and women, even as it works to define with greater clarity the difference between ministry and vocation. We have reason to rejoice that the church bodies which merged to form the ELCA were led by the Spirit to ordain women. Women have many gifts to bring to the ordained ministry. Now we must work to assure that the church understands ministry, and defends zealously the call women have to be pastors. This will be a difficult and challenging process over the next generation. Women, whose ministries in the Lutheran church have been and continue to be many and varied need not think that the only way to serve the Word is to become a pastor. Rather we should celebrate the fact that women can now have vocations in all the offices of the church, from teacher to presiding bishop. Our tradition of understanding both vocation and ministry is rich, as this book of essays shows.

2

There Are Many Workers in God's Household

L. DeAne Lagerquist

Lutheran women? Surely there have been some. Certainly they have been busy doing their appointed tasks in the church. I'm convinced of it by reason and personal experience; but the written record of the Lutheran church often has failed to mention either that women were present in the church or what they were doing. The cast of characters in the various accounts of Lutheran history are not unlike the people mentioned in the standard historical accounts of other Christian churches. Until the past quarter century women were strangely absent.

Generously interpreted, this oversight can be attributed to a particular way of looking at the church. In its extreme, this view takes leaders of the church to be representative, if not constitutive, of the church. Thus the church's history is well told by attention to leaders and their concerns. Additionally, leaders are understood to be those persons who are called, trained, and ordained to the office of the ministry. Consequently, women don't appear in the history of Lutheranism in the United States until at least the mid-20th century, a time when women began to assume more public roles in the church.

There are, however, other ways of looking at the church and other ways of identifying its leaders. When local congregational historians reflect on the life of the church, they give consistently more attention to the activities of women than do denominational historians. In the local setting it is difficult to avoid seeing women and their contributions to the congregation; in contrast, photographs of denominational meetings taken as late as the 1950s make it obvious that women were not there to be seen.

Another way of looking at the church is to consider some of the images suggested in the New Testament. Three very diverse images include a fortress, a ship, and a bride. Each implies the proper work of the church's members. If the church is like a fortress, then the members are engaged in defense of the treasure which the fortress protects. If the church is rather a ship, the members of the crew are busy with sailing about the world to deliver their precious cargo. If the church is a bride, its members carefully prepare themselves to receive the bridegroom.

Lutherans recognize these images in stained glass and hymn texts; nonetheless Lutheran ecclesiology is not primarily imagistic. A concise and valuable statement in the *Augsburg Confession* describes the church as "the assembly of all believers among whom the Gospel is preached in its purity and the holy sacraments are administered according to the Gospel" (Article VII, *The Augsburg Confession*). This description is central to Lutheran identity and must be taken into consideration in any discussion of the church in a Lutheran context.

An interpretation of Article VII which places emphasis upon the purity of the preached gospel and the proper administration of the sacraments, those two tasks which define the office of the ministry, contributes to the view that the church's history is the history of the clergy and their concerns. (See also Article V, "The Office of the Ministry," *The Augsburg Confession*). This is the view of the church which has been blind to the presence and roles of women. There is, however, more to the *Confession's* description of the church than preaching and administering the sacraments. The church is "the assembly of believers." Attention to this phrase and its companion, "the priesthood of all believers," shifts the focus of the description to the people. From this

perspective, the church's history includes much more than doctrine and polity. The life and piety of the "person in the pew"
is taken seriously as worthy of scholarly consideration.

Such a move is consistent with recent developments in Christianity and historiography. The documents of Vatican II refer to
the church as the people of God, retrieving a major New Testament image. In the past quarter century the laity of many Christian churches became more active and assumed increased responsibility for their churches. Similar developments, such as the
American civil rights movement and feminism, have prompted
historians to study "people's history" and to do history from this
point of view. Attention to the women and other people who did
not appear in earlier historical accounts has increased.

In this brief and preliminary essay, I will look at another image
for the church, and show how the church is well represented as
the household of God. This image has strong biblical support.
It is in keeping with current concerns for the whole people of
God. It is consistent with the confessional description of the assembly of believers. And it is particularly appropriate in the Lutheran context as the Reformation restored the family household
as an acceptable setting for Christian life. What the image conveys
about the work of the members is particularly well suited to the
topic of this essay. It does not begin with elite leaders who hold
offices; rather, it provides the opportunity to consider the tasks
carried out by all persons, and in this case, women in particular.

Behind the decision to begin here is the assumption that each
member of the household has been given a talent, a skill, or a
charism (gift) which is to be used in the doing of some task for
the service of the household and its head. It also follows the
process by which specific offices were developed in the early
church; tasks and functions preceded formal offices. To begin
with, the notion that the ministry of the church is carried out by
clergy obscures the ministry done through the service of the other
members of the household. Looking at the service of women
identifies and highlights other tasks which might then be considered as offices or forms of ministries.

What have women done in the household of God which we call the Lutheran church? They have prayed and sung, they have raised money and contributed where there is need, they have cleaned and fed, they have learned and taught, they have mourned and rejoiced. Lutheran women have done much. In the past century and a half they have often done these things through women's societies which are discussed elsewhere in this volume. A smaller, but significant number of women have done these tasks as deaconesses.

I propose to tell about what women have done in the church under four types of service. Women have served through their gifts of hospitality, patronage, teaching, and administration. Each type of service can be found in Pauline admonitions concerning the use of gifts and life in the Spirit: hospitality, Rom. 12:13; patronage, Rom. 12:8; teaching, Rom. 12:7b; and administration, 1 Cor. 12:28. When I refer to the women who do these things I have chosen to use the gender identified terms _patron_ and _hostess_. In the first case, the feminine term _matron_ conveys something quite other than what I intend. In the second, although _host_ is sometimes used to refer to women, I prefer to emphasize that the task of hospitality has frequently been carried out by women.

We must recognize at the outset that the specific examples of women and their activities which I cite are primarily illustrative. Much primary research remains to be done. Consequently there can be no pretense of providing the definitive treatment or interpretation.

The materials available to me are almost exclusively about women in Lutheran churches in the United States. This limits the geographical and chronological scope of this essay. I am able to mention a few European women in the decades of the Reformation. The Lutheran women in other parts of the world, in Brazil, Namibia, or India, for example, are absent from this essay despite their work in the household of God. Without them this story is incomplete.

This is one telling of the story as it is now known from historical research. On the basis of this evidence I suggest a revised view of the church and of leadership which will allow us to see the contributions Lutheran women have made to the church. Once women's presence and activities are recognized, their contributions can begin to be evaluated. I anticipate that the contributions of female members and leaders which can be seen from this shifted perspective will raise questions that are relevant to contemporary discussions of ministry.

The Gift of Hospitality

Prior to the Reformation, Christian women in Europe, particularly noble women, were able to withdraw from the obligations of family to pursue holiness in a religious order. There women had clearly defined religious careers through which they could contribute to the church in a valued manner. The Protestant reformers' rejection of monasticism removed this option. While men who might have become monks retained the possibility of becoming clergymen, women had no such alternative. There was no formal role for them in the Lutheran churches. The newly esteemed family was the arena of many women's lives. Variations in the scope of Lutheran women's activities appears to be primarily attributable to their class and to the status of women in their society.

Women's task of hospitality in the household began early and endured into the late 20th century. Women saw to the basic needs and the comforts of family members and visitors. In 16th-century Germany, Ursula Cotta was reputed to have taken in the student Luther and given him food and lodging. In recognition of her contribution to the reformer's career and to evoke similar generosity, the women's organizations of some German-American congregations called themselves "Ursula Cotta Societies."

Katherine von Bora, wife of Martin Luther, demonstrated this essential gift of hospitality. As mistress of the house, she provided for her own family and for the hordes of students and visitors who passed through her door during their stay in Wittenberg.

The parsonage continued to be a particular place of hospitality. On the American frontier the pastor's wife was hostess to her husband's traveling colleagues, to confirmation students, and to assorted others who required her service. Similar hospitality was also offered by other members of the congregations. The itinerant pastor found his bed and board in the homes of scattered parishioners; no doubt it was the women of the house who prepared both as they did for touring choirs and youth groups in later decades.

Hospitality was not limited to homes. It extended into the life of the congregation. Women served food at joyous and tragic occasions shared by the people of the parish. Without diminishing the pride the cooks and bakers took in the quality of what they served, the value of their service was perhaps less in the food and more in the opportunity they created for the members of the household to gather. At wedding receptions, anniversary open houses, and funeral luncheons, hospitality provided the occasion "to rejoice with those who rejoice and weep with those who weep" (Rom. 12:15).

Women were also responsible for the appropriate setting for worship. In American churches, long before there were church buildings, women provided their prized tablecloth to cover a makeshift altar and their crockery to serve as communion vessels. Often, it was the women who saw to the decoration and cleaning of the church. They made communion wafers. They filled and washed communion cups. As organists, choir directors, and singers, women contributed to the music of worship.

Most of the hostess tasks in the church, so like what women did for their own families, were done solely by women. Of all the tasks, the musical ones were most often shared with men. Hospitality assured the members of the household of survival and comfort. The hostesses of the church gave the household of God a service which is essential.

The Gift of Patronage

Closely related to hostesses are patrons of the church. The same women have frequently done both tasks. A patron is one who protects, fosters, or supports. A patron is a regular customer. In the first sense, a patron is one who gives; in the second, one who receives. Lutheran women have been both. They have been regular participants in worship, hearing the gospel preached and receiving the sacraments. The composition of the Sunday morning worshiping community today makes it obvious that women have been, and are, patrons of the church in the second sense. The value of what they receive and its worth to them is a complex topic and too important to treat here in a superficial manner.

The sense of a patron as one who gives is multifaceted, encompassing several sorts of support. A patron protects and defends by lending power and status. Noblewomen such as Bavarian Argula von Grumbach provided this sort of patronage to infant Lutheranism. Fostering growth is another way of being a patron. Many women did this by being baptismal sponsors. In this action they fostered the growth of the church and of the individual whom they sponsored. A patron uses her influence to advance the fortunes of the object of patronage. Anna Børs, wife of the Norwegian consul, exercised this sort of patronage for the benefit of the people of Brooklyn in the late 1800s. She cooperated with male leaders of the Norwegian-American Lutheran community to bring Sister Elizabeth Fedde to New York to institute deaconess work.

Patronage suggests financial support. Børs was a patron in this sense as well. She pledged the funds required for Sister Elizabeth's work. Other women were equally generous with their material resources. Ingeborg Homme's inheritance was the capital to begin a cluster of institutions in Wittenberg, Wisconsin. A Mrs. Troutman from the Ohio Synod paid the expenses of a man preparing to be a medical missionary in India. Miss Betora Matsen paid Sister Milla Pederson's salary for one year so that she could return to her work in Madagascar. Other women donated lots for church buildings or cemeteries and houses to be parsonages. The role of women's organizations as financial patrons of the church is well known. In the case of American Lutheran churches, the financial support of women's organizations was vital to the transition from tax-supported state churches to voluntary denominations. Although patronage of all types is not an exclusively female task, it is one to which women have made remarkable contributions.

The Gift of Teaching

In the course of fostering the growth of the church and its members, women have exercised gifts of a third type, as teachers. The audiences for women's teaching varied from their own children, to college students, to members of congregations. The reformers' stress upon the importance of knowledge and understanding, as well as belief, gave teaching an important place among the tasks in God's household. Within the family, parents were charged to educate their children in the basics of Christian teaching. Luther provided the *Small Catechism* to aid them in this, but he did not assign responsibility specifically to either fathers or mothers. In practice, mothers often took the initiative for the religious education of their children both by formal instruction and by providing a model of pious life.

In the United States, Lutheran women extended their teaching from their own children to those of the congregation in Sunday schools. Single women also instructed children in special weekly classes or summer religious schools. The movement of women into these volunteer and paid positions was closely related to the Americanization of the original immigrant members.

Continued development of religious education stimulated a need for materials. At first, the junior departments of churchwide women's organizations provided programs. Later the church publishing houses cooperated with appropriate units to produce materials. Frequently the authors were women as were the teachers who made use of the programs.

Although some churchfolk argued that women ought to teach only children and other women, they served as teachers of college and seminary students as well as of adults in their own congregations. In the 19th century, prior to the establishment of a school for the training of Norwegian-American pastors, Diderikke Brandt assisted her husband by instructing young men in languages. Bertha Paulssen taught sociology to students at Gettysburg Seminary from 1946 to 1962. Many women taught on the faculties of Lutheran colleges. Their acceptance of salaries lower than they could have commanded at other schools was an indication of their motivation and commitment; they preferred to do their work at a school of the church. In recognition of the influence of such teachers, St. Olaf College has named buildings for Agnes Mellby, Agnes Kittlesby, and Agnes Larson, and Wittenberg University has named one for Margaret Sittler Ermath.

Women contributed to the ongoing growth of their congregations by teaching adult classes. This activity was first cultivated within the women's organizations which urged women to take responsibility for their own programs. Many women used their knowledge and skills to the benefit of their congregations as teachers of the Bethel Bible Series. Further indication of women's commitment to and influence on the educational aspect of the church's life was seen in the efforts of American Lutheran Church Women which prompted development of the Search Weekly Bible Studies used in thousands of congregations in the 1980s. Certainly teaching is not a gift limited to women. Nonetheless, women's contributions to the life of the church as teachers, both as instructors and examples, has been substantial.

The Gift of Administration

Tasks of a fourth type come under the heading of administration. These are tasks which contribute to the smooth functioning of the household. They are fundamental to the work of the other members. The patron and the hostess sometimes slipped into the role of administrator. Certainly a woman such as Katherine von Bora was not only a gracious hostess, but also a competent administrator in the running of the Luther home.

Administrators, like teachers, were more likely to be paid workers in God's household than hostesses and patrons were.

Deaconesses ran large hospitals and schools of nursing in the service of the church's ministry of healing. Female missionaries took charge of schools and health care facilities. Mary Markly was appointed by the United Lutheran Church as the first female full-time executive in 1919. She was one of two secretaries for student work, a relatively new field of ministry. Following World War II, Cordelia Cox's administrative gifts were crucial for the success of Lutheran World Federation refugee resettlement programs. The effective work of women's organizations also depended upon the competent administration of their leaders, women such as Katherine Lehmann. In 1986, Kathryn Baerwald was elected General Secretary of the American Lutheran Church, and Dorothy Marple was the principle staff person for the Transition Team which oversaw the beginning of the Evangelical Lutheran Church in America. Throughout the 20th century the church's dependence upon the work of women such as these grew as the number of women in executive and support positions increased.

In congregations the work of women in two areas was particularly significant. The parish secretary's work, volunteer or paid, was crucial to communication among congregation members, to their worship experience, and to any number of aspects of parish life. Most often this work was done by a woman who provided continuity between several pastorates and oriented newly arrived clergy.

After the mid-20th century, women served on the boards, church councils, and committees of their congregations. As members of these bodies, women contributed their administrative gifts. This volunteer service extended beyond the local church into its regional and national manifestations. However, formal positions, such as church council officers and church executives on the national level, have been filled by men more frequently than by women.

Summary

This brief discussion of Lutheran women as workers in God's household is more concerned with the participation of women than with their exclusion. It highlights some of the tasks women did and continue to do rather than focusing on what they have not been permitted to do. Taking this positive approach allows women to be recognized for their contributions and given credit for their work. It also raises two clusters of questions for current discussions of ministry. The first set concerns the significance of the tasks women have done in the church. If it is true that the gifts of hospitality, patronage, teaching, and administration are beneficial to God's household, then provision should be made so that these gifts are cultivated. As the roles of women and men in our society shift, who will be the hostesses, patrons, teachers, and administrators of the church?

The second set of questions relate to the implications of women's past contributions for women's work today. How are current perceptions of women's activities shaped by women's previous tasks? What is the significance of the services women have given in the past to contemporary women as they consider their own ministries as laywomen and clergy? Do they value the contributions of their foremothers or disdain them? When women use their gifts as workers in God's household today do they continue and expand the work which women have done before?

3
Being at Home in the Church

MARY HULL MOHR

A bout seven years ago, I was asked to give a speech about women's service in the church and so I spent a considerable amount of time thinking about the subject. At the time, my mother, who was 79, was living with me, so it was natural that I reflected on her lifetime of devoted involvement in all aspects of church work. My mother was a pastor's wife and was very comfortable in all aspects of that role as it was defined during the 40 years of my father's ministry. The role of pastor's wife meshed beautifully with her talents. An accomplished speaker, she was often called upon by other congregations to arrange and present programs at women's meetings or banquets. Until her final illness, she liked nothing better than to arrange and present such programs, whether for an ALC Women's program or a mother-daughter banquet. She had an excellent memory for names, genuinely cared about people, and kept in touch with everyone's joys and sorrows.

My mother's special interest in the church was missions. Her one regret about the merger in the '60s was that the Lutheran church to which we belonged would lose its Women's Missionary Society. In every congregation she accepted leadership positions in the society. Although she refused to accept such positions in the "Ladies' Aid," as it was then called (believing that the women in the congregation should develop their own leadership abilities in that organization), she wanted to be directly involved in the Women's Missionary Society.

When I finally gave my speech in 1979, I organized my thoughts around the concept of the public and private church. My thinking about my mother's role had made me aware that women had been very involved in important ways in the work of the church. What church, I asked, were women in the late 1970s very actively complaining about not being a part of? I argued in that speech that it was the *public* church. I was thinking about the role of the clergy in the preaching and worship of the church, the shaping of the church's theology in the seminaries of the church and in its publications, leadership positions in the church bureaucracy: the church that provided professions for men. To this church, women had not had access. But the *private* church, as I called it, in which my mother was a leader, was for many women a very important part of religious experience. In the small towns in which I grew up, it was this church that helped make the institution central in our lives.

Together with the school, that private church provided the social context for all of us. I remember from my childhood a Thursday night supper in our church to which the whole town came. The menu was always the same: homemade rye bread covered with melted cheese, and what was called goulash, really hamburger casseroles of every description. I can still remember the smells of the church hall on those evenings and the warm feeling of togetherness that accompanied the men, women, and children breaking bread together. But it was the women in the church who volunteered to do the planning, the cooking, and probably the insisting that husbands and children attend. My mother would bring her rye bread and her casserole to join the others. Pastors' wives were not excused from helping to provide the great quantities of food that seemed to be a part of the private church in those days.

There were points at which the private and public church came together: women, for the most part, taught Sunday school; they incorporated the majority of adult Bible study done in the church into their organizational meetings (although I do also remember

Lutheran Brotherhood meetings which I presume also did some Bible study). Women considered the study of the Bible and the teaching of the young an important part of church life. They attended church on Sunday morning and knew that such worship was central. But they also saw the life of women's church organizations as important and the work that they did there as vital to their religious experience and their service in the church.

Seven years ago, when I described the life of the public church, I was thinking mainly about the role of the clergy. Even at women's meetings a very special place was reserved for the pastor. And to be honest, my mother lived and worked in a kind of reflected glory because she was married to a pastor. One of the most difficult adjustments that she had to make when my father died was to no longer think about herself as the pastor's wife. The pastor represented the church in a way that no one else did. There was a way in which the historical church was carried on in those congregations through the pastor. Women's work changed over the years, but the pastor preached the gospel, which was unchanging. He had been educated in a way no one else in the congregation had been, and because of that education and ordination, he was the authority on most matters, including those that affected women's organizations.

I was very much aware in 1979 that it had been impossible for me to find a role model in my mother for my own life in the church. For one thing, I did not marry a pastor. But even if I had, my life in the church would have been different. Like so many women my age and younger, I had spent my adult life either in school or working. I had neither the time to give nor the interest in the kinds of organizations to which my mother devoted her time. But there was another part of the public church which very much had provided a role model for me. For although women could not be pastors, there were other kinds of occupations available in church institutions. I had been born in a hospital owned by my church, my best friend in early grade school was in a children's home owned by my church, I took music lessons at a college owned by my church, and a good friend had a mother who was a matron of a church retirement home. The occupations

of nurse, teacher, administrator were all roles that could be filled
by women in church institutions. Many women also were on the
foreign mission field doing similar tasks. So although a woman
could not be a pastor, it was very possible for her to find employment in one of the church's institutions. Obviously, there
were also jobs in the church itself for women. The title "parish
worker" often covered being a combination secretary, education
coordinator, youth worker, choir director, and organist in the
church, and many women saw these positions as opportunities
to serve their Lord.

When I began to think about employment for myself, then, I
followed the model that was closest to me at the time: teaching
in one of the colleges of the church. I went to a college owned
by our church. There I had a woman teacher, Henriette Naeseth,
who had a profound influence on me. She inspired me to go to
graduate school, and she was my connection to the Lutheran
college in which I now teach. It was through her, and later
through other older women teaching with me, that I understood
that college teaching could be a way to serve the church. If I had
been a man, I think I would have become a pastor, but I saw
teaching in a college of the church as a very logical way for me
to become a part of the church's work.

If I were writing my speech today, I do not think I could so
easily make a distinction between the public and the private
church. It may have been a useful way to think about the church
of my mother's generation, but no more; and perhaps not even
a useful distinction for those women. Certainly my mother had
never thought about her work in the church as being any less a
part of the larger world than that of my father, although if pressed
she might have said that his work was more "important."

Another distinction that I made in the late 1970s may be more
to the point. Women, including me, were reacting at that time
against what we saw as "women's work." The jobs that women
could do in the "public" world, even the world of the church,
were "women's" jobs, such as nursing, teaching, and secretarial
work: the so-called nurturing professions. Women had been allowed to participate in those areas that were basic to the development of the person, but men in those professions had managed

to keep to themselves such high prestige jobs as doctor, superintendent of schools, pastor. Women reacted strongly to being stereotyped in such a narrow set of occupations.

Much has changed in the last 10 years. Not only are women becoming doctors, pastors, and school leaders, but they are also becoming part of those aspects of society traditionally thought to be the domain of men, such as business and government.

What does this mean for the church? The changes in the last years do not just have to do with women's paid employment cutting into the time available to be in the church organizations or even with the new roles which women have assumed, both inside and outside of the church, although these changes are significant. The changes have the most to do with the nature of the church as an institution and the church's relationship to our life in society. Since to do justice to this topic would involve writing a book, I wish to discuss here the church's relationship to its nurturing institutions and suggest that it is time for women to think about how our traditional roles can help us to fashion a new future of service in the church.

How is the church changing? In 1980, I was asked to be a member of the American Lutheran Church's Committee on Church in Society, and served four years as its chair. That committee had just been formed when I became a member. Its very name and the office which it oversaw and advised suggested something new about the church's role. We met several times a year to discuss the problems of the world: poverty, hunger, nuclear disarmament, the farm crisis—the list could go on and on. Some of these issues were approached in the traditional ways. For example, the problems of hunger were addressed through the institutions of the church, as was the mission program and Lutheran World Relief; but on many of the issues we served as a kind of link between the church and other institutions of society, e.g., the federal government. More and more I felt the pull between the church and the larger society.

Because of my committee job, I was asked to serve on the Task Force on Society for the new Evangelical Lutheran Church in America as well as a study group for Lutheran World Ministries.

Many of the conversations in these two settings exhibited the tension between thinking of ourselves as supporting our own work in our own institutions and becoming a leaven in the life of the larger society.

Since I am still a member of the faculty at one of the colleges of the church, I have also observed this subtle shift firsthand. Although it is probably true to say that the colleges, at least those affiliated with the former American Lutheran Church, still feel a close identification with the church over and against state-owned and other private colleges, the ties with the church are not as close as when I became a faculty member some 25 years ago. And there are clearly a few people both in the church and in the colleges who would like that relationship to be severed completely. I've wondered what this means for the way in which women serve the church.

Another theme that has echoed in my consciousness as I have served on church committees and study groups during the last years is the word "lay" member. I suspect that my mother never thought of herself as a "lay" member. Certainly she would never have thought of herself in the ways in which that word comes up these days. For when I hear it, I usually hear those of us in the pews being asked to share in the responsibilities of the clergy. I have wondered (not very charitably, I am afraid) if this emphasis on stressing the responsibilities of the "lay member" coincides with women becoming clergy in the Lutheran church. In any case, when I hear the term, I wonder about what it is I am supposed to be doing in response to my Christian commitment.

The short answer to that question is that I should be living out my life as a Christian in whatever situation in which I find myself. Or, as Martin Luther argued, the calling for a Christian can be realized in any kind of work. The thoughtful person, however, needs more specific guidance. On the one hand, does one's connection with the institution of the church just become attendance at Sunday worship with a willingness to take one's turn in the running of the institution? Or does being a Christian wherever one is simply mean doing to others as we would have them do to us? And what about those people who really wish to serve in the institution of the church, but who don't want to be clergy? In the first blush of women becoming clergy we forget that for many, men as well as women, the kinds of skills necessary to be effective in that calling are not the talents everyone possesses.

I wish I had the kind of guidance that many are looking for. I can only hazard some suggestions based on my own experience. First, I believe that the church should not get rid of its direct involvement in institutions other than the church, expensive though that involvement is. I still feel that the range of occupations that a church can offer its people and the kind of service those people can give is an important contribution for the church to make both to the people cared for and as a model to the larger world of what service should be like. Since my own experience has been in a college of the church I will use the church's work there as an example. A liberal arts education for post-high school-age young people comes at a crucial moment in the development of lives. These young people are seeking a direction for their adult lives, and need the atmosphere of sophisticated theological education and guidance in the questioning of faith that such colleges ought to provide. The communities that such colleges of the church can foster can serve as models for young people in their own shaping of their lives with others.

The federal government's involvement in hospitals and social work has probably meant that the church's role can never again be what it once was in those fields, but it is still important that the church maintain a presence in these organizations both on staff and on institutional boards. The traditional institutions of the church were the basic caring ones, and the church has a stake in those that goes beyond its association with business and government.

But these institutions are for those who see a paid life of service associated with the church. For most women such service will still take place as volunteers. It is therefore necessary to think about how we can become directly involved in the institutional work of the church. And here is where I think women need to build upon their traditional gifts (and include men as well, wherever possible). Women can become teachers in the churches in some new ways. More and more we are seeing the fragmentation of our society; by that I mean that the institutions of our society do not mutually support each other. This is, of course, one of the consequences of living in the kind of pluralistic society that the United States is. Sociologist Robert Bellah noted in *Habits of the Heart* that citizens have a decreased sense of commitment to the greater whole in a society such as ours that stresses individual development so strongly. If the church is going to have the kind of impact on society that it wishes to have, then the institutions of family, church, and education need to be interdependent.

It logically follows from this, I suppose, that I should counsel church-supported elementary and secondary education—and yet it is also true that such an education further fragments our society. It should be possible for a strong church and family structure fostered by that church to be one of the shaping influences in the school system of a community without imposing religious beliefs upon those in the school. What this means is a church which becomes very active in the issues that affect the local schools and a church educational system that pays more attention to school curriculum in its attempt to complement that curriculum. Such an agenda for a church would interest many women (and men, I hope) as they seek for some sense of wholeness and community in their busy lives.

Women should also not be afraid to use their experience as homemakers in the church. The church needs to become more of a home to its members. The church was a natural home in the small communities in which I grew up, but that sense will have to be carefully cultivated in today's more complex and urban society. And we will then need to redefine who will be the "homemaker." Many women in the past found it fulfilling to use their "homemaking" skills for the family of the church. Women of my mother's generation had the right idea of how to take people into the church and make them part of the larger family. Wasn't this just an extension, they thought, of how one makes someone comfortable in one's home?

Some real tension now exists in the church around these home-making tasks. Should one follow the pattern of the working woman and just hire the cleaning and cooking tasks done? Should women who work outside the home be excused from participating and those women who have retired or who are full-time home-makers assume these duties? Should men and women share equally in these tasks and the women's organizations become men's *and* women's organizations? If we lived in an ideal world, people would joyfully perform those tasks for which they felt suited. Since Lutherans, of all people, should understand human failings and the kinds of resentments that can come from what many consider inequity in doing these tasks, we need to have serious conversations within our churches about how the family building and maintaining tasks of the church are to be carried out. It will be easier to carry on those conversations when we think of such tasks as more central to the mission of the church than many now do.

How can women serve? I like to think of the church of the future as being a kind of home base, a place in which one's life is centered. Increasingly our society has tried to convince us that the family is such a place, but as families change and become more mobile and smaller, and as the traditional family increasingly becomes a thing of the past, the family becomes even less able than before to provide us with the kind of "homes" that we need: places to which we can go for strength and sustenance. The church can be such a place. Obviously, being a homemaker involves our thinking about all aspects of the lives of the people of God.

Besides being a vital worship place where the gospel is preached and the sacraments are administered (and this must remain the heart of the church's mission), this church could become more of a social and educational place. Here we could come to know the other people who worship with us, both in our own congregations and in congregations around the world. Women have the skills, I think, to create a community in a congregation that not only helps members to find support for individual lives, but which also helps them make a commitment to the task of the church in the larger world. And we need to do more thinking about the church's relationship to that world. This can only be accomplished through a very active educational program for adults. More would be required than our Sunday morning study groups.

But what of the organizations that many women still find important? In my church of the future, these would become more task-oriented. I think my mother's experience still has some validity here. She was passionately interested in foreign missions, and the organization devoted solely to that work gave her the most fulfillment. It should be possible to develop a number of task-oriented groups, which women (and men sometimes?) could join, and which would have beginning and ending times. I think many women would find such groups fulfilling and would find time for them.

I have been richly blessed by the opportunities which I have found to serve the church. Perhaps it has been more continuous with my mother's service than I have thought. She never had a paid job in the church, but she worked in many different ways, through the gifts of the Holy Spirit which she had been given, to strengthen the family of believers. In her time, her way of doing this was effective. The world changes, and we must adapt our service to that world. But our goal of "homemaking" remains the same. We can use the special gifts we have as women to make homes for our "family" in our individual parishes and in the larger world.

4

A Heart for the Heartland

A CONVERSATION

WITH ANNE KANTEN

Anne Kanten is proud to identify herself as a farmer. She grew up on a farm in Iowa, along with a sister and two brothers. A strong family heritage shaped the Knutson children. One brother, Kent, served as president of the American Lutheran Church from 1970 until his death in 1973. Another brother, Gerhard, is bishop of the West Central Wisconsin Synod of the Evangelical Lutheran Church in America. Anne says of her sister Mildred who has raised eight children, "She is an activist, a mover and shaker in church and community." Anne married a farmer and they reared a family of three children on a farm in southwestern Minnesota. Presently Anne is the Assistant Commissioner of Agriculture for the State of Minnesota.

I went to the Agriculture Building in St. Paul to speak with Anne and had been in her office for only a few minutes when she pointed to three pictures on the wall:

Anne Kanten: In the center is a picture of the farm. That piece of land has been the bridge between four generations of Kantens. It is land that has meant commitment to place and community. It is land that has produced a life-style of strength and identity. It is land that has given us a dependence upon the most profound of gifts—life, growth, rebirth—for to be a farmer means that you live with these miracles everyday.

Our son Kent and his wife Kim are the fourth generation on that land, and for their sakes, and the fifth generation, and the sixth, we, like other farm families, must talk about sustainable agriculture. It is because of future generations that the land issue has become central to American agriculture.

The second picture on the wall was given to me by a friend when she came back from Brazil. It shows the Brazilian farm family huddled in a ditch with their backs against a barbed-wire fence, the result of corporate expansion and export agriculture, and below, in Portuguese, it says, "The land is God's, and the land is for all people." That picture asks the basic question, "Who is gaining control of the land?" One thinks not just of Brazil and Latin America, but of our own heartland, our farm families.

The third picture I brought back from a trip to South Africa, and it shows a myriad of faces on which you can see the frustration, the agony, and the desperateness of people. The young artist who did that picture entitled it "Who Is Going to Speak for Us?" American farmers, 2% of the population, also ask that question. "Who do we trust in the system?" "Who is there who really cares about land and its quality?" "Who cares about the people who struggle there?"

Marilyn Preus: These pictures give me some idea of how important land is to you. For years we have called rural America the heartland because it has provided stability for our culture as well as supplied our physical needs. In recent years, radical changes have occurred in farm communities which have threatened the security of farm families, and the rest of society. What most concerns you about the present agricultural situation?

AK: Today both the land and rural culture are in deep crisis. A recent USDA [United States Department of Agriculture] report shows that in the next 20 years the United States will lose over a third of our last remaining topsoil. Over two-thirds of our nation's farmland is losing topsoil at a rate faster than nature can replenish it. Interwoven with this horrible erosion of the soil is the economic crisis facing the people of the land.

Thousands of farm families lose their farms every year. As a result, businesses, schools, and churches dependent on these farms for their economic support, will suffer a severe loss of income. It is possible that over 50% of our family farms will disappear by 1990; 90% will be gone by the year 2000. A number of economists today agree that fewer large-scale operations, approximately 250,000 commercial farms, have the capacity to produce the food needed domestically and internationally.

I am very concerned that we take seriously the gift of land and the responsibility that comes with it. Our land, this earth, is the supreme gift of God, the placenta upon which all life is dependent. If the bounty of this gift is well cared for, there will be abundance for our children. But if it is taken from the many and exploited by the few, injustice will prevail. The land will no longer be cared for, thus denying our children a bountiful future.

I'm not only concerned with what we're doing to the land and its resources, but even more, what is happening to the people. I just spent an hour on the phone with a farm wife who said, "This past year, with its ups and downs, has been difficult. I can't go through anymore. I've cried a lot and I'm at the point where I don't really care if we stay on the farm. . . . I don't understand how people without faith can cope, how they can make it. As far as a family is concerned, this kind of pressure, this kind of hurt will either tear you apart or bring you closer. We are lucky because it has brought us closer together."

MP: What do these rural problems have to do with the church? Or, maybe it's the other way around!

AK: There is a close relationship between the problems I have described and the church. The church has been a stabilizing and unifying institution in rural America. It has been the center, the primary social institution for farm families for centuries. Today it must provide support and care to farm families experiencing massive debts and severe loss.

The erosion of rural culture must, and can be stopped; but it will require the dedicated leadership of Christians who understand the need for justice and careful stewardship of the land. These Christians can lead the church to play a key role in changing government policies and altering moral, ethical, and social attitudes of both urban and rural people. As a church we can give leadership to reverse the rapid centralization of the ownership and control over God's gift, the land.

The church should be involved in rural problems because we have God's Word and God's promise, "And you shall eat and be full, and you shall bless the Lord your God for the good land he has given you" (Deut. 8:10). Walter Brueggemann has written, "The land may be freely given. But it is not freely kept. It is kept only as Israel transforms the land into an area of justice, righteousness, mercy, and fidelity. Unjust people will lose land. There are not enough policies or strategies to resist God's unsettling will for justice. The loss of land is neither mechanical nor is it mysterious. It happens in terms of political processes and realities. So it may be an invading army (Hos. 7:9), or it may be a usurping, confiscating economic arrangement." (*Dialog* 19 [1980]:170) The church acts in time of agricultural crisis because Christians understand that justice among the people of the land must exist alongside a caring for the land itself.

First of all we have to remember *we* are the church, no matter where we serve. If it is a political appointment, such as mine, no matter what the job, we are the church. We serve with our convictions and our faith and our beliefs undergirding what we say and what we do and how we address the problems. That's probably the way the church can be the most effective.

I believe the church *must* be involved and I've sometimes run into a lot of static because of my convictions. Many folks say the church has no business in political arenas, addressing basic policy issues. But the gift of land is the church's business, because land is from God.

Christians have been involved in justice issues for a long time. They were there with abolitionists. . . in the Civil Rights struggle. . . and in peace movements; but somehow in agriculture we are afraid to take that step, to be prophetic. To me, the people of faith can risk. We don't have to calculate the percentage of probable success. We are faced with a tragedy of unmeasurable proportions as we watch the depopulation of rural America. It is time the church takes a prophetic stand in the protection of land and landed people because it is a matter of justice.

MP: From your observation, how have people in rural America, and women in particular, lived out their Christian commitment during this critical time?

AK: I guess that answer is as varied as there are churches and congregations. My friend Kathy who belongs to a church in a small community says, "We never talk about it in circle, though we sit there together and many of us have the same problem; but we won't talk about it. Oh, the pastor does pray for those who are in economic stress, he prays that things will get better. . . ."

Let me tell you about another friend of mine who in her own way was beginning to help her neighbors by sitting down with them, getting their papers in order, making them feel more confident when they walked into the lender's office. Her name is Lou Ann Kling. She came to me one day and said, "I can't continue to do this. I can't pay the telephone bill and buy the gasoline to drive to see my neighbors." Out of that conversation was born the Minnesota Farm Advocate Program which is now a cadre of 25 farmers. They have been trained by expert lawyers in the complexities of the farm credit system and FmHA [Farmer's Home Administration] regulations, bankruptcy law, tax law, federal farm law, state farm law, and everything else a farmer must know. It is absolutely incredible today—the rules, the regulations, the information that a farmer must have to make any sort of decent decision.

A farm advocate is trained to sit down with a farm family to explain the regulations that virtually control a farm family today, to explain options under the law, to do accurate cash flows for the lender's desk, to help prepare farmers for the mediation process when farmer and lender meet to restructure debt, to be a friend—a true advocate, to see what there is in the systems of government and in local communities to help a farm family in stress today. It is a peer relationship, farmer to farmer, one of the most beautiful and successful programs now in the state of Minnesota. That service is free to the farmer. It is supported by our state legislature which now pays some of the expenses so that advocates can serve to their fullest. Since that program began in March 1984, those farm advocates have helped over 12,000 Minnesota farm families. And it was begun by one woman!

Dianna Hunter, one of these advocates says, "The farm problem is a complex entanglement of concerns: political, social, economic, environmental, and spiritual. The issue of justice threads through it, including the hunger of the Third World. . . the issue of survival threads through it, too. Agricultural chemicals, industrial waste, and the use of our natural resources have combined to threaten the earth's ability to sustain life. . . . [Women] have the capacity to act now and take the power of love and faith into the society. . . seeking a healing and rebirth of our rural communities."

I have observed that women bring a special kind of tenacity and compassion to the farm crisis. It is a time, I think, for us to be at the forefront of the crisis we face, because we recognize the interdependence between the family on the land and the environment. I think of the many times the kids and I have had to deliver baby lambs and how we've struggled to save a lamb, just to help it be born. Sometimes we have breathed into their nostrils until we see the lungs begin to work. And there have been times we haven't succeeded and we experienced death. All is a part of being a farm family.

Tenacity and compassion are illustrated in the film *Country* where the farmer's wife dealt patiently and lovingly with a spouse who was very discouraged. She helped the kids to understand what was going on and be patient with Dad. She supported the neighbors who were hurting and she attempted to get people to talk together. She kept the family records and went to the lender's office to defend their own operation. And on the day of the auction sale, she said to the lender, "You can come and take the machinery and you can come and take the livestock, but when you come and take the land, you better bring more than a piece of paper." It's that kind of tenacity and commitment that we must have, and we do have, as rural women today.

Back to your question. So much of the strength of the church has come from rural congregations and small town congregations where faith is tied to strong ethical and moral principles. While one must be careful not to romanticize life in the heartland, extolling rural values and virtues unrealistically, we must recognize that in the past the church has been the primary social institution in rural America. This connection has shaped values, life-style, and attitudes toward authority. Rural people committed to living a life that is basically good and kind, within the limits of the law, have often found it difficult to challenge the system, even though in our hearts we know the system to be unfair and unjust.

I remember back in 1977 when it was a part of our strategy as farmers to strike, to stop the actual production of food. It was a movement that began in the southern part of the U.S. and swept up through the North in the spring of '78. I remember how hard it was for me to pin a button on my farm cap that said, "I am on strike." I was not comfortable opposing the establishment. I had gotten the message that it was difficult to live out a Christian commitment in the political world. This was not an arena for nice folks, certainly not for women. I wanted nothing to do with it. I think there are a lot of rural women who had gotten the same message: "The political arena's not for us." This kind of thinking made it hard for us, as rural church people to say, "I'm angry," to say, "I will take a stand against policies and systems that control us."

I think the women's organization in the church has done a number of good things to help women understand themselves and the crises we face. Perhaps what we need to hear from the church more than anything else is, "You're free, free to participate, to be political. Stand up and speak your convictions and your faith, what you believe to be right and true and just. Your voice is as important as any other voice of power."

The church, and specifically the women's organization, was my training ground. Here I learned to deal with differences of opinion, to write resolutions, to say what I thought, to express my faith publicly. Group Bible study was the place where I found it safe and comfortable to say what I thought. This closeness to the church brought me to platforms to speak about the stewardship and the care of land, to say that as farmers, as farm women, we need to care about that gift, that we have an awesome responsibility to that gift. But then I began to realize that we have a responsibility beyond the care of the land. The church must have a concern for the people who live and struggle and attempt to remain as stewards of the land.

The reaction was mixed. Sometimes it seemed that people in the church didn't seem to understand at all. When I started to talk about my concerns they called me a radical. Somehow I had become political and no one was very sure that had a place in the church. I was angry. I felt disappointed and let down. Many people in the church didn't seem to care what was happening in agriculture. They didn't understand how policy changes would be devastating to the land and water resources, and to the people themselves.

But there were some positive experiences. One special person was our bishop, Darold Beekmann. He listened and understood and made us feel like our voices had a place. This encouraged me at times when I felt alienated from my church.

And there were also times of unexpected church support. I remember a day when a number of us chose to support a family facing foreclosure. This family lived 50–60 miles north of our farm. They had been dealt with unjustly by the lending agency and so there was a group of farmers who were going to the lender's office to say this injustice must stop. For me that was scary, but it was something that had to be done. And I went along with the group. I remember walking into the lender's office and finding the Lutheran pastor and probably 30 or 40 people from their congregation there. It was absolutely overwhelming for me! I was so moved I remember fighting back the tears. I just hadn't seen my church on the "cutting edge" before.

This story shows that people matter. Our policies are obsessed with the idea that we can build bigger tractors and bigger discs and bigger plows and then we can produce food with fewer people. But somehow, we forget that we can't build communities and schools and churches and hospitals without people. As people of faith and stewards of the land we must speak out against injustice. It is time for another Amos. You remember what he said. "Hear this, you who trample upon the needy, and bring the poor of the land to an end, saying, 'When will the new moon be over, that we may sell grain? And the sabbath, that we may offer wheat for sale, that we might make the ephah small and the shekel great, and deal deceitfully with false balances, that we might buy the poor for silver and the needy for a pair of sandals, and sell the refuse of the wheat?' The Lord has sworn by the pride of Jacob: 'Surely, I will never forget any of their deeds' " (8:4-7).

It's time for the church to be prophetic. We have nothing to lose. That is our role as the church, to stand and speak for what is just and what is right. After all we are dealing with God's gift, God's gift of creation and it's not ours just to mess around with. We are here to be participants in creation, because creation is a continuous process and we who live on the land are a part of that process and we aren't to be harassed or destroyed because we've figured out how to build bigger machines and a better technology.

MP: Anne, you are passionate about this subject! How did you develop such deep concerns for the land and the people of the land, and what shaped your religious convictions?

AK: My parents came to this country from an island in the North Sea, where it was my father's task as a young man to take a bucket and climb among the rocks and look for dirt to expand their meager potato patch. He went to sea at 14, and 15 years later, jumped ship in New York to visit Uncle Jacob in Iowa and when he arrived there he was overwhelmed to find rich, black topsoil—several feet deep. He decided to stay. Dirt made me an American!

I grew up on that precious piece of land, along with my sister and two brothers. I got the message that church and society were separate and later had to learn the hard way that Christians are meant to be *in* the world. Mom seldom went to town; she was never comfortable with the language. Dad bought the groceries and attended school events and served on political committees to "fix what was wrong." The men talked of war, policies, farms. Women were not involved. My brother Kent was three years older than I, and it was clear to me that "he was in charge." It took me a long time to figure out who I was. I felt socially awkward in school. I was a scared country kid, with a conservative, naive look at the rest of the world; but I had a literature teacher who cared about me and encouraged me to go to college.

I became a teacher and loved my career very much. During that time I met Chuck, a farmer who had a very deep appreciation for land and the history of family on land. We were married in 1952 and together we established new roots on a piece of land. The '50s and '60s were a very difficult time for farmers. The price of our commodities went down. There were a lot of upheavals. I remember when women and children stood on the road to block livestock trucks; but I was not involved, I was afraid. I didn't think that was my place; instead I was taking care of the family.

The early '70s were different; it was just fun to be a farmer. Prices were up. The world was hungry. We were told to produce fence row to fence row. Optimism abounded. Lenders were anxious to lend money on inflated land values. But then in 1976 there was a drought. I remember we sat around the kitchen table hour after hour and talked about our farm and our future. I could see clearly the hurt and stress and fear in Chuck's face.

Realizing that the church must be concerned about the land and its people, I began preaching on land stewardship. I took to the road to talk about what was happening to farm families. In December of 1977 we made our first trip to the state capitol, with a number of farmers, to say, "There is trouble in the land." In January 1978, Chuck and I went to Washington, D.C. I remember him saying to me as he looked around at 30,000–40,000 other farmers, "We are not alone!" It was then I really knew the depth of his agony and his hurt. That's what the church must be saying to our hurting communities now, "You are not alone." The church can help to bring the pain and divisiveness to the surface. As a church we are good at making all kinds of statements to get groups and committees and conventions together; now farm families need support and a clear sense of their worth.

Jesse Jackson at a youth convention some years ago said, "Stand up and say, 'I am somebody.' " I feel like doing that at farm meetings. As farmers, we need to say that to each other. So often we see ourselves as powerless people, swimming upstream against the giant grain corporations, the banking systems, the economists and the government bureaucrats—those who tell us, "We know what's good for you," and they continue to write policies that destroy us.

I asked my friend Bev to testify before a Minnesota legislative committee, and she said, "We've lost our dignity as rural people, as food producers, and we have become beggars—beggars for operating money, for loan extensions, for debt restructuring. We feel harassed, humiliated. We feel we have failed."

MP: Anne, women serve God, serve the Word, in many ways. Do you think of your position in state government as a calling?

AK: Yes, I do. I serve in a state-appointed position and I see it as a calling. Even though this calling came from a political arena, it's the way I live out my Christian commitment to serve to the best of my ability. God gives us good heads, a venturesome spirit, and sometimes a bunch of courage to venture forth to do what we have to do. There are many times I'm scared to death by the awesome responsibilities on my desk, but I pray a lot and go!

Today is Monday. I just had a phone call from my boss asking me to be in Washington on Wednesday to testify before the full Senate Agriculture Committee. That's scary; but I'll do it.

There are many heavy responsibilities in my job. The whole regulatory division of the state department of agriculture is under my desk. That means that I deal with the dairy division, the grain division, the agronomy division, the plant industry division and food inspection. That's more than 200 people with a great deal of technical expertise.

But "there is trouble in the land" and we have a tremendous opportunity and responsibility, as concerned Christian people, to be a part of bringing about a new age where we talk about societies preserving and cooperating and creating rather than abusing and competing and destroying. I think it's a challenge for us to restore creation for the service of all God's creatures.

I am a farmer and I am a woman, the first woman to sit at this desk in the department of agriculture. And I am also angry. I am angry at systems and policies and profit motives that allow millions, mostly women and children, to die because they are hungry and thirsty, and then those same systems and policies tell me as a farmer I must face bankruptcy because I produce too much food. I am angry at economic systems and international food policies whose strategy of cheap raw material has resulted in chronic low prices around the globe and has destroyed farmers, not only in this country, but farmers on every continent.

We must begin to care about one another. One more story. There was a small island in the South Pacific. On that island there were two villages, one high on the mountain, one down on the shore. One morning the mountain villagers woke to see a huge tidal wave rushing toward the island. They knew it would destroy the village and their friends on the shore, but there was no time to run down to warn them. So they set their village on fire, knowing and trusting that the families on the shore would see the flames and run up the mountain to help, and both groups would survive.

We must begin to care about one another. We need the voices of women from every sector: we need them in the church, from the pulpits, from the women's organization, from the committees; we need them in the political arena, on the township level, on the county commission, in state government, in Congress. We can help to restore new life to the heartland.

5

A Heart for Service:
The Lutheran Deaconess

E. LOUISE WILLIAMS

They say if you are very quiet you can hear your own heartbeat. That may be true. However, for deaconesses over the years, it has not been especially easy to hear their own heartbeat, for several reasons.

First, deaconesses have been mainly doers and actors, very attuned to the heartbeats of others, especially the heartbeats of the neighbors they sought to serve, but they have not been accustomed to being quiet enough to hear their own. Second, in the church's discussion and description of ministry, two heartbeats have predominated: one, the loud heartbeat of the ordained clergy; the other, not quite so loud, the heartbeat of the laity. Third, deaconesses have seldom spoken for themselves. Male pastors or bishops have most often spoken *for* them and *to* them; as a result, we know more about what others thought the diaconal heartbeat was or should be than about what deaconesses themselves think about it.

In the past dozen years on the staff of the Lutheran Deaconess Association, I have listened to the heartbeat and experienced the ministry of deaconesses in a special way. More and more I hope that every woman who looks at the diaconate can see something of herself expressed in it and can feel her own heart resonate with what is there. More and more I hope that every Christian, female *and male*, will recognize that they pulse with the same heartbeat, heard most clearly beating in the servant Christ.

Theological Heartbeats

As I have studied the theological and scriptural basis for the ministry of deaconesses, I have come to think about three images still embodied in today's diaconates. The first two have been typical of the traditional roles of women in both church and society, comfortably accepted by the powers that be. The third has not been quite so well accepted.

1. Waiting tables

Diakonia, the Greek word from which we derive "deaconess," means at the root, "to wait tables." To serve at table is to nurture, to nourish, and to be attentive to another's need. It means not only waiting *on* but also waiting *for* the other person, being patient to learn about the other person's likes and dislikes, to catch the sign and signal that service is required or desired, to be available without interfering, to be helpful without being too visible. Being a good table server means being courteous and allowing "the customer to be right."

A Greek table waiter also tasted the food before it was served, to make sure it was tasty, and more importantly, to make sure it was not poisoned. A table server's life was on the line, ready to be sacrificed so that the one at table could live.

Another aspect of waiting table for the Greeks was to cater a feast. This meant not just being concerned with serving individual needs but also making sure that all the guests had a good time, with enough to eat and drink.

Some would say that this picture of diakonia describes the role women have had in church and society. They would go on to say that today no self-respecting, liberated woman would want to see herself in such a role. Deaconesses have felt this tension in themselves and within their communities. In the last decade or two there has been a lot of discussion about service and what that means.

To be a servant can be a problem if women, or any other oppressed people, believe they are expected to do these things by others who exert power over them. When this happens there is no freedom for real servanthood, only powerless slavery. It makes a difference how one is called to serve. And it makes a difference whom one serves.

It also helps us to understand what it means to be a servant when we recall who sat at table with Jesus Christ: the poor, the sinners, the outcasts, those who are the "least of these." To be a table server in the New Testament sense, therefore, is not to be subservient to the powerful. Rather, it is to serve the servants and give them the nourishment essential for life. Not only women are called to be servants, but the whole church is called to follow the table-serving Christ, the one who tasted our food, who risked death that we might live, and who hosts the Eucharist feast for us.

2. Washing feet

A basin and a towel have long been symbols for the diaconate. They call to mind the picture of Jesus washing the disciples' feet, showing them how they are to serve one another (John 13).

Washing feet is humble service, on bended knee, awkward, sometimes backbreaking. It is coming into contact with what we would rather not touch, the dusty, smelly, blistered parts of humanity. It is personal, even intimate. The service of footwashing is shaped by the other's need as the towel is shaped around the foot.

I was first stimulated to think about the "towel tools" of *diakonia* by reading Walter Brueggemann's book, *Living Toward a Vision: Biblical Reflections on Shalom* (United Church Press, 1982, pp. 135ff.). A couple years later I attended a seminar for pastors, mostly men, who were discussing this book with Brueggemann. They talked about how frustrated they were using these pliable "towel tools" for ministry. They said they would rather have tools that make physical changes in things, tools like the ones carpenters use: hammers, saws, vises, screwdrivers. The group seemed unresponsive when I suggested that perhaps they could better learn how to use those "towel tools" by listening to and watching women because women even today are likely to be washing feet: of their children in bathtubs at home, of the sick in hospitals, of the elderly in nursing homes, of the dying in hospices.

Like most other women, deaconesses know about washing feet. And we know, too, that this kind of service puts us in a vulnerable position where someone can kick us and where we cannot easily run away, there on bended knee.

Footwashing, like waiting tables, can be oppressive if we are relegated to that task or if we choose it because we think that is all we are worthy to do. But it takes on a different meaning when we think of Jesus. He had the option of equality with God but did not hold on to it, clutch it, or hoard it, but emptied it out, taking on the form of a servant (Phil. 2:6-8). Jesus became like us in every way and calls us to serve one another. When we do, we are changed, for in our neighbor we meet Jesus who said that when we serve the least of these, we serve him (Matthew 25). His life has redefined the ministry of the church, and given it the heart of footwashing service.

3. Working for change

Back in the old days when people operated with a simpler view of the world, *diakonia* was a bit simpler too. It usually meant personal service to people you knew, extending yourself to respond to a need that was obvious, serving "the poor" whom you could touch. It is no longer quite that way. *Diakonia* has been broadened to include a concern for the whole creation, to working for justice and dignity for all.

For the past 20 years the World Council of Churches has discussed what this new concept of *diakonia* might mean in the life of the church. It has been especially crucial because the diakonia of the church has long been focused on "works of mercy," perhaps particularly embodied in the large diaconal institutions especially throughout Europe. A 1982 report of a consultation of the WCC on *Contemporary Understandings of Diakonia* emphasizes that *diakonia* today must be concerned with the structural and political dimensions of social problems.

Today any theological picture of the diaconate must balance the table-waiting and footwashing images with working for change. This kind of service does not fit so comfortably with traditional women's roles. It means standing on tiptoes, not just on bended knees, using every ounce of expertise, competence and power we have. It means stretching ourselves to the limits of our gifts and going to places where some would say we do not belong: to the seats of power in government or church, to work for a more humane world, and to do all we can "so that the (Reign) of God which is still to come in its fullness can be related to the present as a foretaste of eternity" (WCC, 1982). Deaconesses and other women have not always been so comfortable in this kind of service. But I believe we are learning, and our theology of *diakonia* is becoming more balanced and the diaconal heartbeat is becoming healthier. The one who ushered in the reign of God and announced its presence calls us to be God's agents so that the reign of God may also come among us.

Historical Heartbeats

When I was a deaconess student in the '60s, I was invited to look at the scriptural references to deaconesses. I had learned to quote proudly Rom. 16:1, "I commend to you our sister Phoebe, a deaconess. . . ." The Greek word, *diakonos*, here translated "deaconess," is the masculine form of the noun variously translated "helper," "servant," "deacon," in the New Testament. In line with the movement to differentiate words by gender (actor/ actress, master/mistress, host/hostess), the masculine form in Greek became "deaconess" in order to refer to deacons who were women. We don't know who Phoebe was or what she did, and we don't really know whether she was a deaconess with a small "d" or a capital "D." We only know that Paul considered her important in the life of the church.

As a student I was also directed to 1 Timothy 3 where we find a list of qualifications for deacons and "the women." Some scholars believe that those women were deacons; others believe that they were merely deacons' wives. Whichever interpretation one chooses, it is clear that they had responsibilities in the life of the Christian community. The qualifications for "the women" is almost identical to those of "the deacon" except that for the women the admonition to "not be greedy of filthy lucre" is omitted. Evidently the women did not dispense alms or handle the finances of the congregation.

I felt a bit embarrassed then that there was so little scriptural support for the ministry of deaconesses. It wasn't until later that I realized that the New Testament doesn't provide a clear definition of any ministry of the church, including the pastoral office. Rather, the New Testament presents a picture of a young church left with the mission and ministry of Christ without clearly defined instructions about how to structure itself to carry it all out. What we see in the New Testament is a picture of ministry that is somewhat fluid, taking different shapes depending upon the particular needs of the church. And there is good evidence that women, sometimes called deaconesses or ministers, had a part in that ministry already in the first centuries of the church's history.

While there are many references to deaconesses and other women in the writings of the early church fathers, historians have tended to discount their importance. I am grateful for those who have begun to unearth the treasures long hidden so that we can begin to celebrate the women, some deaconesses, who laid important foundations for us.

In the post-apostolic church, the diaconate thrived, and the male and female diaconate were almost parallel, taking shape in response to the church's needs and the constraints of the patriarchal society. Deaconesses were involved in two areas of work, works of charity and liturgical functions, often doing those things which male deacons or bishops could not do. They were considered the agents of the bishop as they visited sick women in their homes (men could not do this), assisted with the Baptism of women (it would have been immodest for male bishops to anoint a woman's breast with oil and immerse her), presided over the women's section of the church (checking the credentials of all who entered to keep out spies and pagans during a time of persecution), accompanied women when they needed to appear before the bishop, visited the martyrs in prison (where men were not permitted to go), and instructed women catechumens.

Especially in the Eastern church the female diaconate flourished. Deaconesses founded and administered schools, became noted biblical scholars, and some were even canonized.

Reasons can be found in both church and society for the decline of the female diaconate after the sixth century. The ministrations of men were less restricted. There was a growing hierarchical understanding of the ministry of the church, with the higher offices absorbing the functions of the lower, and the male diaconate becoming a prerequisite stepping stone to the higher offices. Baptism of adults became rare, and men and women were integrated in worship so that the liturgical functions of women for women were not necessary. The decline of the Roman Empire also made it unsafe for women to live and work alone, and deaconesses began to live in groups which eventually became cloistered and adopted monastic ideals. During the Middle Ages, ministry to the poor became less important as the church became preoccupied with individual salvation, ascetic practices, and theological problems.

On the one hand, the history of the female diaconate during those early centuries typifies the way the church became increasingly male-dominated while women were relegated to the tasks which men either did not wish to do or were unable to do because of cultural restraints. One might ask if we wish to continue to use the title "deaconess" with all this historical baggage.

But there is, I believe, another way to read that history, to reclaim some of it, and to see there positive foundations for the diaconal heartbeat that continues today. It is remarkable, given the developments of the church, that women were involved in ministry at all. Perhaps what is most important is to see that

women were teaching and ministering to other women. I wonder
if, in those early classes of catechumens, women told their own
stories, supported each other and celebrated each other's gifts
the way 20th-century groups of women do. I wonder what it did
for women's self-image to have women teach them or to see a
woman standing beside the bishop at Baptisms and representing
him in daily works of mercy.

The female diaconate remained dormant for a very long time.
While the theology of the Reformation was more compatible with
the heartbeat of the diaconate, nothing significant developed until
the mid-19th century in Germany. I became better acquainted
with that part of our history in 1975 when I attended a meeting
of Diakonia, the World Federation of Diaconal Associations and
Sisterhoods. The assembly was held near Beilefeld, Germany, at
Bethel, one of a number of diaconal centers founded during the
19th century revival of the diaconate as a way for the church to
respond to the grave social problems arising from the Industrial
Revolution and subsequent urbanization.

Pastors in Germany had a dream of an "Inner Mission," in-
corporating both evangelism and social action as means for re-
newing the church and society and responding to the needs of
the whole person. Out of this Inner Mission grew a variety of
charitable institutions, children's homes, orphanages, hospitals,
rehabilitation centers, schools, mental homes, and others. Since
these institutions needed dedicated staff to accomplish the important work, it seemed a natural move to "restore" the female
diaconate. But this restored diaconate was different from what
we saw in the early church. It was not an office established by
the church, but rather a sort of order of unmarried women living
a communal life in a motherhouse and serving primarily in institutions of mercy. How loudly the diaconal heartbeat must have
beat in those years! There were thousands of deaconesses
throughout Europe. The motherhouses, even though always directed by male pastors, still provided space for women to be
educated, to have a voice in their own governance, and to exercise
leadership in ways that would not have been accepted in the
society at large.

While in Germany, I visited a number of deaconess houses, to see their work, and to talk with sisters who had given their whole lives to serve those in need. I sensed the echo of the heartbeat that had been there so many years before. I saw many beautiful examples of service to hurting people. At Bethel there was a marvelous mutuality among the "staff" and the "clients" who were often considered throwaways by society: people with severe developmental disabilities; people with brain dysfunction because of uncontrollable epilepsy; transient, unemployed men; and others. The heartbeat was still there. But the strength of the heartbeat was fading. Many of the deaconess houses had more sisters in retirement than in active service, and most had no candidates in training. The institutions that had been built and the communities that had been formed as such a creative and appropriate response to human need now stood as barriers to change in a new age.

Deaconesses first came to North America in 1849 when four German women came to Pittsburgh to work in a hospital with Pastor William Passavant. In 1884, seven more came to Philadelphia at the request of John D. Lankenau. By the turn of the century there were hundreds of American deaconess groups, primarily living in motherhouses and staffing hospitals and other charitable institutions. For the most part they were organized outside the official church structure.

The founding fathers (and they were all fathers) of the deaconess movement on this continent would not seem especially progressive to us today; still they were seen as *avant garde* by many in their era. It wasn't easy to convince others that it was a good idea to have women in ministry. There was a concern that these religiously trained women would not "keep their proper place" or that the whole idea sounded too monastic or that somehow woman's "highest calling," to marry and bear children, would be undermined.

But the needs outweighed the concerns. The diaconal heartbeat was there, and the women served faithfully, often without much official recognition or status. Wearing grey or black or blue or brown garb, they went about their work quietly in hospitals, orphanages, schools for the deaf, homes for the developmentally disabled; and those whom they served noticed something in them—the heartbeat of the servant Christ. If you talk to older Lutherans, you will hear a story here and there about the powerful witness of "Sister _____" or "Deaconess _____." The history is impressive, and for a time the movement flourished in the United States.

Like their European counterparts, many American deaconess communities found it hard to adapt to the changing needs of the church and world. Health care and social services became more professionalized and more the prerogative of the state rather than the church. Women were confronted with expanded educational and vocational opportunities inside and outside the church. Living in a motherhouse, wearing garb or uniform, and remaining celibate often seemed unattractive to young women, even those highly motivated for Christian service. Most diaconal communities found they had fewer and fewer students and more and more aging sisters who had been promised life-long care.

In the mid-1970s I visited the Lutheran Deaconess Community (ALC) in Milwaukee shortly after they had made the painful decision to close their doors. I listened in awe as the sisters, some in their 90s, told me their stories. They knew about waiting tables and washing feet and working for change. They had done this for a long time and they had found much joy and fulfillment in their lives of service. They expressed bewilderment and sadness at two things: first, that it seemed young women were not attracted to this same selfless service; second, that the church seemed so unappreciative of them and their service. They could hardly believe it when I told them that the Lutheran Deaconess Association had over fifty students.

Our generation was a different breed of deaconesses, and some of the elderly sisters might have wondered if we were real deaconesses. We hadn't operated with a motherhouse since 1943, I told them. We worked primarily in parish ministry in areas such as religious education, youth work, calling on sick and shut-in members, music, social ministry, counseling. If we worked in institutions, it was usually not as nurses or matrons, but as chaplains or social workers. We received salaries and often lived alone. Remaining single was not required; we even had several married students.

The form was very different, but as we talked across the generations, it became clear that the heartbeat was the same. It's not always loud, the numbers aren't great, but if you listen carefully, you can hear it still in contemporary Lutheran deaconess groups: the Deaconess Community of the Lutheran Church in America, Gladwyne, Pa.; the Lutheran Deaconess Association/Conference (a free-standing, inter-Lutheran organization) in Valparaiso, Indiana, and the deaconess training program (Lutheran Church–Missouri Synod) at Concordia College, River Forest, Ill.

Future Heartbeats

Does the diaconate have a future? Is it still necessary, now that women can be ordained as pastors? Isn't it irrelevant now that Lutherans are working to reaffirm the ministry of the whole people of God? I believe the diaconate has an even richer future because the laity are becoming more conscious of their ministry and because there are women pastors.

While the whole church is called to a life of *diakonia*, the diaconate is sometimes a particularly appropriate way for the church to do its task of waiting tables, washing feet and working for change. Deaconesses are *doers of diakonia* with a special care for those most easily ignored, forgotten, and undervalued: the imprisoned, the ill, the young, the old, the dying, the bereaved, the homeless, the poor, the disabled, the unemployed. Deaconesses are also *enablers of diakonia:* assisting, affirming, equipping, and supporting others as they respond to Christ's call to service in the world.

The diaconate is also a sign in the midst of the church, a living reminder of the servant Christ who calls us in our Baptism to be servants in the world.

In all these ways, the ministry of the laity, the whole people of God, is, I believe, strengthened by a strong diaconate. In like manner, the diaconate is enhanced by the ordination of women to the pastoral ministry.

The ordination of women challenges the diaconate to listen for its own heartbeat and to articulate more clearly what that heartbeat is. Both Scripture and history show that deaconess ministry is one of many expressions of ministry in Christ's church, not something women can do because they cannot be pastors. Women who enter the diaconate today have made a clear choice for the ministry of *diakonia*. They have considered other options and have determined that the diaconate is truly their vocation. This will surely strengthen the diaconate.

Ordaining women pastors has raised for fruitful discussion, but not yet for definitive answers, the question of membership of men in diaconal communities. Asking and discussing this question can only be healthy for us.

Lutherans on this continent still need, in my opinion, a broader understanding of the ministry of the church, an understanding that makes room for a variety of forms and uses a diversity of gifts. Surely the diaconate will be enriched by such an expanded sense of ministry. But the future of the diaconate does not depend upon ecclesiastical decisions or recognition. Rather the future of the diaconate is rooted in and grows from the faithful response of Christians to the call of the servant Christ. As long as Christ calls and people respond, the diaconate will survive and serve. And the heartbeat will go on.

6

Volunteers: A New Challenge for the Church

MARLENE WILSON

My earliest memory of serving in my church is still very vivid. As a small child I helped my mother when it was her turn to clean the church in the small Montana town where I grew up. How I polished and shined the pews, the altar, and communion rail, and what a sense of awe and purpose I felt, even as a child. This was my church and I had a part to play in keeping it beautiful.

As I look back on my journey of volunteer service to the church since that time, my story could be Everywoman's, or at least the story of Lutheran women who are forty or older: Sunday School teacher, nursery attendant, ALC Women's (or "Ladies' Aid") officer, Bible school and Bible study leader, youth sponsor, funeral and wedding committee member, a worker in the altar guild and at bazaars, pot lucks, lutefisk dinners. The list goes on and on.

The most amazing thing to me is not that we have done all of these things; it is rather how seldom we, or the pastor and male leaders of the church, have viewed it as ministry. Even though we have added some new options of service for women in many of our Lutheran churches, i.e., church council, usher, social action committee, liturgist, to name a few, we still have not understood this service as a valid form of ministry. It is merely "helping out," "taking our turn," or what we do because "no one else will do it this year."

The Lutheran church is rooted in three powerful biblical and confessional concepts that help us to understand volunteer service as ministry: the priesthood of all believers, not just the ordained; the whole body of Christ, with each member given a special purpose; the giftedness of each Christian which elicits our faithful response (Romans 12). Given this tradition, we can regard volunteer service in and for the church as legitimate ministry.

A Look at Societal Trends

I have been actively involved in the volunteer community for the last twenty years, first as Director of the Volunteer Center of Boulder County and later as an author, trainer, and consultant for non-profit organizations and churches. I have conducted seminars and workshops for over 60,000 people on the topic of volunteer management in all parts of the United States and Canada. My observation is that the church is basically ten years behind other organizations in effectively utilizing, organizing, and appreciating the service of volunteers.

Often I have encountered women in the leadership positions of community voluntary organizations who tell me that they tried first to share their gifts and leadership talents in their churches and were not well received or accepted. They felt pushed, rather than sent, into the world to do what they were able to do. And they feel a great sense of sadness about that. "Why can't I give my best gifts to my own church?" is the cry of many women I know. Why, indeed!

This dilemma has prompted me to focus approximately one-half of my time on the issue of using volunteers effectively within churches. I work not only with Lutherans, but United Methodists, Presbyterians, Episcopalians, and Catholics as well. To translate what I have learned from secular voluntary programs into church settings, I wrote a book, *How to Mobilize Church Volunteers* (Augsburg, 1983).

In workshops and seminars for churches, one of the things we deal with is the tremendous effect of societal trends on who is volunteering, who is not, and why. A few of these trends are:

1. 45% of the adult population of this country today are "baby boomers," between the ages of 25–39.

2. 70% of the women in this age group work outside the home.

3. The most important value of the baby boom generation is participative decision making, that is, being involved in decisions affecting them.

4. There is presently a "baby boomlet," that is, baby boomers over 30 are having their families.

5. For the first time in United States history there are more people over 65 than there are teenagers. 2.5 million people are over 85.

6. By survey, 70% of people in the United States who claim church membership are not actively involved in any service within the church.

7. Only 7% of American families are "traditional" families, that is, the first marriage with children still at home.

John Naisbitt, in his book, *Megatrends*, had identified many more significant trends; but for the purposes of this topic, these are some of the most important.

What are some of the implications of these realities on women's involvement in the church? We must struggle with these issues honestly. Let us look at some of them.

When we consider the average age of women participating in Lutheran women's groups, we must conclude that these groups do not often include women between the ages of 25–39, the baby boomers. Why? Too often these groups meet only during the day when 70% of the younger women are at work. The opportunities to serve the organization are mostly in 1–3 year terms which is a long-term commitment for working people and single female heads of households. They can more easily say "yes" to 3–6 month projects and shared jobs. The different age groups are interested in very different program issues. The younger women long for help with two-career marriages, single parenting, stress and time management, while the older women are more likely to want socialization and small Bible study groups. Both sets of needs are legitimate, but different. We need to do programming that meets the needs and realities of diverse groups.

The baby boom women who are having their families later are, whenever financially feasible, frequently opting to stay home for a year or more before going back to work. Many of them have 10–15 years invested in a career and have enormous skills to share. What an exciting opportunity for our churches to tap into this incredible reservoir of talent! Churches which provide competent day care make it possible for women to use their skills in challenging assignments.

How can we in the church define leadership so that success is measured not by how many hours we put in and how many different jobs we do at once, but by how many others have been involved with us? The idea that the chairperson is the one who does all the work is counter-productive.

Remembering that participative decision making is the number one value of people between the ages of 25 and 39, what can we do to involve these people in the decisions affecting their own lives?

Women, as well as men, are retiring younger and living longer. They have skills and are in better health than even before. Considering their ability to serve in significant ways, how can the church program *with* and not *for* seniors?

Why are 70% of church members not actively involved in volunteer work in the church? This is getting to the heart of the matter. In interviewing many of these "pew-sitters" we have found they consistently list these reasons for uninvolvement:

1. The jobs in the church are almost never adequately defined in writing, so they are not sure what they are being asked to do.

2. The leaders of the church often use terms like "we never do that here" or "we always do that here," whenever new ideas are offered, giving the new person the clear message of not being needed or wanted.

3. Clergy and lay leaders too often do not know how to delegate well, that is, share their work with others in a significant and meaningful way.

4. If people are asked to do something, they are asked, not because they have gifts for the task, but because someone is needed to fill a slot, i.e., "I've called ten people and you're the last on my list."

5. They fill out time and talent sheets year after year and are never called.

6. Too often they are not given choices: what they would like to do and do well, what they do not like to do, what they would like to learn and when they need a sabbatical to keep from burning out. Many of today's pew-sitters were leaders in another church at one time and are burned out with over-involvement, so now they sit and watch.

A Word About the Word—"Volunteer"

Two words commonly used in speaking of lay involvement in the church are *volunteer* and *disciple*. Sometimes, in an effort to describe what we are doing, we may have become caught up in one of those word games that diverts energy from doing something about lack of lay involvement to arguing about what we call it. The result has been the dismantling of some very exciting and effective training for congregations to help them deal in a practical way with the declining involvement of the laity.

In secular circles, the word *volunteer* is used to designate those who give their time, commitment, and talents to a cause without monetary reimbursement. The word helps delineate those people (volunteers) from the paid professional and support staff in the organization. Thus terms like "paid staff and volunteers" or "paid and unpaid staff" are often used. It has been a most necessary and helpful way of understanding work responsibilities, relationships, policies, and procedures. It has helped the two groups know better how to function together as a team.

The word *volunteer* is used in a similar way in the church to distinguish between duties of paid and unpaid workers. There is an added dimension, however, and that has to do with the "why" of any Christian's involvement, in the church or society, paid or unpaid. Christians who know themselves to be called to follow Jesus view their volunteer work as discipleship, done out of a sense of obedient commitment to their Lord.

In my opinion, the church has a long way to go in helping its members understand the term *discipleship*. The church can be aided by effective volunteer training which will help to move people from the idea that they are "taking their turn" to seeing the opportunities for "using their gifts"; from thinking of themselves as "last on the list" to valuing themselves as unique children of God; from the notion of service in the church as the duty of a few to understanding that ministry as discipleship belongs to the priesthood of all believers.

Volunteer Ministries

1. To the church

In a frequently quoted article entitled, "The Day the Volunteers Didn't," Erma Bombeck envisioned all of the vital services to communities, hospitals, schools, youth organizations, etc. that would grind to a halt if volunteers did not show up. It was a powerful image. I would suggest that Erma Bombeck's fantasy is a worthwhile exercise for us to do as we view the life of the church, or a single congregation. We can best understand the enormous contributions women make to the life, health, and vitality of the church if we envision what it would be like if all of that service were suddenly withdrawn. What a bleak picture that would be!

I believe the biggest challenge we have is not so much changing the ways women can serve, although we do need to work on that as more and more women develop skills in the workplace; it is rather changing the ways the church looks at their service. How can the church, and women themselves, see volunteer work as valid ministry which is as precious in God's sight as that of ordained and paid staff? (This is an understanding which lay*men* need as well!)

2. To the community

A vast number of women are involved in meaningful volunteer work in the community, i.e., Girl and Boy Scouts, Red Cross, hospitals, nursing homes, emergency housing and feeding programs, literacy efforts, child and wife abuse shelters, to name a few. Very seldom is this work acknowledged by their churches. In fact, they tell me that sometimes it almost seems to be resented if it takes them away from "real" church work.

Here is an enormous challenge for the church. How can women acknowledge as well as celebrate this vital activity and see it as serving "the scattered church?" How will women feel sent out on behalf of the church? How will women understand this volunteer work as discipleship at its finest?

3. To the women themselves

Three of my favorite authors are Elizabeth O'Connor (*Eighth Day of Creation; Search for Silence; Journey Inward, Journey Outward*), Madeleine L'Engle (*A Circle of Quiet, Walking on Water*), and Mary Schramm (*Gifts of Grace*). All three of these women write eloquently about the theology of gifts and the tremendous importance of discovering our gifts if we are able to be fully the person God intends us to be.

> We ask to know the will of God without guessing that his will is written into our very being. We perceive that will when we discern our gifts. Our obedience and surrender to God are in large part our obedience and surrender to our gifts. Because our gifts carry us out into the world and make us participants in life, the uncovering of them is one of the most important tasks confronting any one of us. (Elizabeth O'Connor, *Eighth Day of Creation* [pp. 14-15].)

> If we confess our gifts, we are apt to be asked to use them. In the end, the sin we must all come to look at is the sin of withholding

ourselves. This is the sin that keeps us beggars in life. (Elizabeth O'Connor, *Search for Silence* [p. 23].)

Live as though you believe that the power behind the universe is a power of love, a personal power of love, a love so great that all of us *really* do matter to him. He loves us so much that every single one of our lives has meaning . . . that's the only way I can live. (Madeleine L'Engle, *A Circle of Quiet* [p. 64].)

Few pay attention to the Christian message if it is not embodied in lives that radiate joy (not a plastic Christian smile, but real joy!). It is easy to distinguish these people from those enduring a life filled with oughtness. To perform a ministry from anything other than a sense of joy is to offer my brother and sister a cold, resentful heart. To be ministers by using the gifts with which we are blessed is authentic discipleship. (Mary Schramm, *Gifts of Grace* [p. 64].)

It has been most often through meaningful volunteer work that women have been helped to discover their God-given gifts and have thereby discovered their unique opportunities for discipleship, both in and out of the church.

Conclusion

Many people are concerned about the present state of the church in this country. They feel that energies are focused on maintenance rather than mission. They are alarmed by declining membership. They wonder about the commitment to discipleship.

Dr. Lloyd Svendsbye, while president of Luther Northwestern Seminary, made these observations: "I see the Christian church in this land opting more for death than for life. Most denominations simply are not hard at work to renew the lives of their own members or to reach the unchurched of this land. . . what the church needs is renewal, not reform. The church needs a sense of new birth, an awakening, a more dynamic relationship to Christ if it is going to have the vitality to do its work and to intersect the drift to the valley of the dry bones."

Renewal in the church would mean a new awakening to what it means to be the people of God, the priesthood of all believers, the whole body of Christ. Renewal in the church would mean a new understanding of authentic and obedient discipleship and a new appreciation for and celebration of the vital role volunteers can and should play in bringing about this renewal. I long for this day!

7

Rethinking the Concept of Lay Ministry

EVA ROGNESS

I am a hospital chaplain. I am not ordained, but I don't think of myself as a "lay minister." I would like to explain what I mean by that.

I was born in Hungary before World War II. My mother was Roman Catholic, my father Lutheran. At that time Hungary had a curious civil law enacted by Hungarian parliament with the permission of Hapsburg Emperor Franz Joseph, which determined that in mixed-marriage homes, where parents could not decide which church the children should be brought up in, the girls were baptized in the mother's church and the boys in the father's.

Every day I received Catholic religious instruction in school. At that age I loved being a Catholic. Aesthetically inclined, I reveled in the rituals, incense, candles, the mysterious Latin mass, and the gorgeous Gregorian chanting. The Corpus Christi festival was my favorite. With other Catholic girls I dressed in white with a flower wreath in my hair, carried a basket of rose petals, which I strewed in the path of the priest carrying the jeweled monstrance (a communion vessel) under a canopy. The streets were lined with people who knelt as we went by, and from time to time we stopped at flower-bedecked altars where the priest did something which I did not understand but was very impressed by. I thought the nuns in their flowing robes were beautiful and I wanted to be just like them. My brothers didn't have anything like that in their Lutheran church!

I felt a security in the power and authority of the Catholic church. In those days they told us what we could and couldn't read. I knew that as long as I did what the church said, my salvation and future were assured.

My father's stance toward the Catholic church intrigued yet threatened me. For generations his family had been part of the small, often embattled Lutheran minority in Hungary, and his own father and grandfather were pastors. In spite of his Lutheran convictions he was close to several priests, and he would go with my mother to mass on occasion, especially if Mozart's music was to be played. But he denied the authority vested in priests and bishops. He talked about living in God's grace and in freedom from the law. He said that no clergy could come between him and God. He asked me why I did things, urging me to wrestle with my own mind and conscience.

We left Hungary at the close of the war, and spent several years in Germany before coming to this country. During that time I read a lot, asked many questions, and in a sense I wrestled with the Holy Spirit and my conscience. With the support of both parents I became a Lutheran at age 15. Our Lutheran pastor was very helpful at this time. He said it was important that I did not think I was "changing from one religion to another," but urged me to be aware and grateful for the nurture I had received from the Catholic church and to appreciate that tradition.

At Augustana College in Sioux Falls I majored in mathematics to become a teacher, but along the way I took biblical and religion courses, studied philosophy, and remember being very much affected by Kierkegaard. I married Michael, a seminary student, and taught school. After he finished, we went to Germany where he began a doctoral program. I also signed up for some theology and philosophy classes. Since women were not ordained at the time, I took the classes for my own enrichment.

Upon completion of my husband's degree and three years in the parish, we returned to Europe where Michael had accepted a position on the staff of the Center for Ecumenical Studies of the Lutheran World Federation in Strasbourg, France. Again I attended courses at the university and conferences at the center, not as an official participant but as a visitor. After three years there we returned to this country and parish ministry in Duluth, Minnesota. For the next 15 years we were immersed in and nurtured by life in a congregation.

One of our children experienced serious illness during those years and we spent a lot of time in hospitals. I learned what it felt like to be a member of a patient's family, what it was like to sit for hours in waiting rooms and hospital rooms and how wonderful it was at times like these to have the support of friends, the church community, and hospital personnel who cared, and to be sustained by the good news of the Christian faith.

In time I felt called to become a hospital chaplain myself. Taking years off from family life and commuting to a seminary toward ordination was out of the question. However, the National College of Chaplains did not consider ordination as a prerequisite, and on the basis of past studies, I was accepted in a certified Clinical Pastoral Education (CPE) program. After completing five quarters of full-time CPE training, I became a staff chaplain at a local hospital. The Lutheran bishop of our district acknowledged my appointment.

I am something of a rarity in the Lutheran church. In the Catholic church there are not only ordained priests, but a large number of nuns and some former nuns serving as regular hospital chaplains. In the Lutheran church, however, I don't know of any other full-time salaried lay chaplains, although there are probably a few.

The most frequent term used to describe my status in the church has been *lay minister*. I am not at ease with that title. Not until I thought through these issues while writing this piece did I learn why the term *lay minister* makes me uneasy.

A Lay Minister

Combining the words *lay* and *minister* does not help define what either word means individually or what they might mean together. The combination is misleading and will inevitably create confusion. People understand altogether different things when they hear talk of the lay minister. What is more unfortunate, the meanings attributed to these words can create division and suggest gradations of quality among the people of God.

What do people actually mean by the term *lay minister*? Often called that, I have listened carefully to what people say and mean when they use this term. This is what I hear:

—"A lay minister is a kind of *mini-minister*, who helps the pastor." They do pastoral work, but are clearly subordinate to the ordained clergy. Pastors do real ministry, but since they cannot do all the work in the parish, the laypeople perform their ministry by helping—serving on committees, teaching Sunday School, playing organ and directing choirs, folding bulletins, ushering, cooking in the kitchen, etc.

—"People are involved in lay ministry whenever they do *church-related tasks* in a congregation or church agency." Theirs is a ministry that contrasts with the ministries of others who work at regular jobs. This assumes a curious distinction between "holy" and "secular" work. If a lawyer spends long hours on a church committee, in the congregation, or on a national church board, we might call that his or her ministry. Does that mean that the regular practice of law that works for justice is not a ministry? Some think of Albert Schweitzer's work in the Lambarene hospital in west central Africa as ministry. Is medical work done in a mission hospital in Africa more special or holy—more of a ministry than what a Christian physician does in a clinic, whether it be in the poverty of the slums or in a well-appointed suburban office?

—"A lay minister is one who serves publicly in the church, which is distinctive from and more special than the private good works of a Christian." For example, some think of parish workers as lay ministers because they are acknowledged publicly as part of the church staff and perform much of their work openly in the congregation. In contrast, a woman in our congregation who baked bread two or three times a week and brought it to some of our shut-ins would not have described herself as a lay minister. Are we going to give different recognition and titles to those who perform 8%, 60%, 40%, 10% of work publicly for the church?

These three interpretations of lay minister are behind my concern about the current trend toward dividing roles of nonordained people into ministries of varying degrees. The problem, of course, is that we agreed to some of this kind of thinking in the merger agreements of the Evangelical Lutheran Church in America (ELCA) which makes it all the more difficult to undo. In addition to the title of Ordained Ministry (ELCA Constitution 10.20), the church also recognizes Associates in Ministry (10.40). They are those who served in the merging churches as Commissioned Church Staff, Deaconesses, Deacons, Lay Professional Leaders and Commissioned Teachers (Continuing Resolution 10.41.A87). Now that the ELCA has been established, no more persons or categories will be added to this roster of Associates in Ministry until a study takes place which will give special attention to "the appropriate forms of lay ministries to be officially recognized and certified by this church. . ." (10.11.A87). Whatever forms these might take, it seems to be an assumption that there *will be* such forms of Associates in Ministry, thus adding to gradations in ministry somewhere vaguely in between and in addition to ordained pastors and nonordained church members.

It is clear that "God has instituted the office of ministry of Word and Sacrament (to which) this church calls and ordains qualified persons" (ELCA Constitution 10.21). But on what basis do we make further categories of Associates in Ministry among nonordained believers? Are some more in ministry than others? Or are some ministries different from others, and must therefore be distinguished by a separate title and category Associates in Ministry?

On what basis will Associates in Ministry be so designated? Do they become so if they serve full-time rather than part-time, or if they are on the payroll of a congregation? Or is it that their ministry is public? Is serving God privately then not ministry? A full-time church school teacher is considered by some as a minister. Nonordained church staff are considered by some as minister, but then the category is split into even tinier pieces when some say that a parish worker or youth worker is a minister, but a nonordained church administrator isn't—presumably because the former group does pastoral work, whereas the second group does more secular work.

This kind of thinking is not biblical, confessional, or at all helpful. If we pursue it to its end, we will end up with a maze of gradations and distinctions of service among the people of God. Some of these distinctions are probably necessary to conform to salary, tax, and pension provisions of civil law or statutes of the church, but they ought not be used in our theological considerations of the church. The minute you create positions, titles, and gradations—human nature being what it is—you start attaching relative values or merits. It is very difficult to resist that temptation.

It is sufficient to say that we all serve in a variety of ways and that pastors have been called to the public ministry of preaching and administration of the sacrament. It is unnecessary theologically to make further distinctions, especially because these distinctions tend to foster inappropriate divisions among Christians.

What, then, is a lay minister?

Layperson

What do we mean when we say layperson? The word comes from *laos* in Greek, which means people. To remain faithful to the original meaning, the word includes both ordained clergy as well as the nonordained, because all are part of the laity, the people of God.

Over the years, we have come to make a distinction between lay (that is, nonordained) and clergy (that is, ordained). What is worse, our mentality has been formed by the popular usage of the word *lay* as nonexpert. We say, for example, "When it comes to medicine, I'm just a layperson." That means, "The physicians are the real experts, and they do the really important medical work." The same with auto mechanics, home repairs, or any other human endeavor. "I am *just* a layperson," as we often hear, means that "I don't know a great deal about this. I might dabble a little, but the experts are the ones who do the important work." Like it or not, that's how people have come to think of layperson in the church as well.

This kind of distinction between lay and clergy is linguistically inaccurate, historically ill-founded and theologically dangerous. The church has been in deep trouble ever since we started using the word laity to mean nonordained people.

You do not find this kind of distinction in the Bible at all. When Paul enumerates the different functions we are enabled to do by the varieties of gifts from the Spirit, that list is inclusive, not exclusive (1 Cor. 12:4ff). We are all included in that list somewhere. Some of us are given this, some of us are given that. Paul uses the analogy of the different parts of the body to emphasize that in this variety they are all part of the one body (1 Cor. 12:14ff.). Here he denies any ranking of value or importance. (In 12:27ff, he does rank apostles, prophets, and teachers as 1, 2, 3, but in the spirit of this chapter this seems to be more gradations of authority or simply enumerations than distinctions of value.)

Psychologically, it makes a difference how we list things. For example, it makes a subtle difference in our thinking when we speak of all the people in the world with their various skin colors as black, white, yellow, red, brown, etc.—an inclusive list—than when we narrow the list to merely two groups, white and non-white which implies that whites are an exclusive group.

When in our daily language we group Christians into only two camps, ordained and nonordained, we tend to widen the gap between laity and clergy. They become exclusive terms, which emphasize there is this special group, clergy, set apart with special training, role, and abilities, and then there is everyone else. Of course the clergy deserve recognition and honor for their service to the church, and the responsibility entrusted to them is very important, but throughout church history whenever rank or hierarchy appears it has been unhealthy for the church. We must not contribute to creating rank or hierarchy by the kind of language we use. When we use the terms *Christian, people of God, disciples,* etc., we are using inclusive instead of exclusive language. Everyone is included in those terms, and they don't constantly keep before our eyes the two camps of ordained and nonordained.

The mission of the church is given to *laos,* the whole church. Jesus' words in Matt. 28:18-20 are a commission to the entire church, as are his words about being witnesses in Acts 1:8. We don't need to belabor the point that the work of the church is entrusted to all.

However, there are some tasks which it would be unrealistic for everybody to do. The church thus calls and ordains pastors to the public task of proclaiming the Word (although we are all witnesses) and administering the Sacraments. Within the Christian community those are specific tasks. Obviously the pastor is not the only one doing ministry in a congregation. The clergy do only a small part of all of the tasks and work of ministry in any congregation.

Minister

The verb "to minister" originally meant to serve, to provide what is needful. The word *minister* is sometimes used in political settings (e.g. Prime Minister) as well as church settings. However, in everyday speech today, more people choose the verb *serve* than *minister.*

Though at one time the two words *serve* and *minister* were synonymous, they now carry different emotional and religious connotations. I serve supper, I serve on a political committee, I serve my neighbor, I serve on the church council. We use the word *serve* in all aspects of our lives: church, state, community, family. Again, it is a nondivisive term, a term that doesn't tend to create qualitative distinctions.

However, the terms *minister* and *ministry* have a certain aura or halo around them. When we apply the word *minister* to a task, we tend to think of that task as something more worthwhile, more holy perhaps, more religious or churchly than when we merely serve or show concern. Have you noticed how reluctant most people are to use the word *ministry* to describe their own actions? A person is more likely to say, "My neighbor ministered to me in my grief," than to say, "I ministered to my neighbor. . ." That, I think, illustrates the emotional overtones and value judgments the word carries with it. Many people would think it presumptuous to speak of their own acts of kindness as ministry, thereby inferring that they were doing something special, perhaps something especially pleasing to God.

We use the word *minister* sometimes in a broad sense, sometimes in a narrow sense. The voguish use of the term *ministry* has stretched it. Here are four ways we use it:

1. We *minister* in the course of our everyday lives, wherever we live and work. We want to serve God in every aspect of life, not only in the jobs we have, but also in our other positions in life: parents, citizens, and so forth. Lutherans have traditionally called this vocation rather than ministry. Ordained clergy are not more holy, nor do they perform more holy work than others, but they are serving God in their vocation as ordained clergy, just as lawyers, teachers, and businesspersons serve in their vocations. This is one of Martin Luther's great contributions to the understanding of Christian life, and we would be better off using the word *vocation* rather than ministry to speak of this broad arena of our Christian lives.

2. We *minister* in our identity as Christians before God. We do not need the clergy as priests, who mediate between the believer and God. We are all priests in that sense, and the more precise term for this is "the priesthood of all believers."

3. We *minister* in the roles and functions we have as members of God's community, the church. We all serve in the church, and in that sense we are all ministers. Some congregations put in their

bulletins: "Pastor: So-and-so. Ministers: All the Members of the Congregation." In the sense that we all serve together in the church, that is true. We need to make clear that ordained and nonordained serve together and collegially. However to avoid making artificial distinction between sacred and secular, it would be much better to use words like serve, care, love, etc., rather than designate gradations in ministry.

4. Some of us *minister* publicly by preaching and administering the sacraments. It seems natural for all of us to use *minister* as a synonym for the ordained clergy. In that case, the term *lay ministry* is invariably confusing. For the sake of precision in thought and language, it would be better to use the term *pastors* or *clergy* when that is what we mean.

Clear as we may be about these four ways of using the term *minister*, we are still not all that clear about what we mean when we talk about lay ministry. It is obvious that we need to do some fundamental rethinking here, and it is bound to take some time. The experience of the Commission for the New Lutheran Church and those committees working with them made this manifestly clear. One of the knottiest questions in the discussions leading to the merger of three Lutheran bodies was this very issue of ministry. It is apparent that we need to spend a great deal of time and theological effort on this subject.

A Woman's Issue?

This issue belongs in the theological discussion of the church. Does it belong in a volume dealing with women's lives? It does.

We need not belabor the fact that the church has historically been male-dominated at the top and in recent American history largely female-maintained on the parish level. The appropriate women's agenda is not to reverse the roles, with the women running the church and the men doing the maintenance. *Rather, it is to make actual what the church is meant to be.*

It is imperative for all the women of the church to participate in the discussions which will shape our understanding of ministry. If we move toward the concept of episcopacy, that is, a church centered around its bishops, and bolster the power and position of the clergy, defining the pastor as someone who is qualitatively different from the rest of the people of God, we would not only be moving away from what Lutherans have understood the church to be, biblically and confessionally, but women, both ordained and nonordained, would lose in the long run. Episcopally oriented churches are those that have historically defined the bishops and clergy from a male viewpoint (Jesus and the disciples being male, and so on) and most are still today adamantly resisting women's ordination and women's participation in church leadership. This system makes qualitative distinctions among the people of God, empowering some to be on top and keeping others on the bottom.

A collegial church model, with an emphasis on the priesthood of all believers, and the laity of all Christians, including clergy, seems to me to be in greater harmony with the teachings and example of Christ. Working together collegially is part of women's heritage. Having in the past been kept out of power structures in several areas, many women have developed "cooperative" working styles, co-op meal sharing with neighbors, co-op baby nursery schools, co-op food stores, co-op quilting groups, and so forth. Women have discovered that working together creates a more receptive climate for nurturing. It would be a pity if we women moved into the traditional power structure of the church for the sake of status and power, instead of helping to reform and transform the structure in ways which would allow the church to grow in grace.

This stance in no way diminishes the true importance of a pastor, nor the reverence and honor we accord them. For we honor them for their loving service and not for their authoritative rule. The authority of the ministry comes from the authority of God's Word and the gift of the Sacraments and not from the persons themselves who proclaim and administer them. I would think such a view would be a great relief to the pastor, a sense of being freed from the burden of having to be superhuman.

What's Next for Me and My Sisters?

How we see the mission of the church and our own gifts will
determine our priorities and how and where we will spend our
energies in the service of God.

There is no "woman's place" in the church or the ministry of
the church. We are all in the church's ministry together. Men
and women combine their talents in any and all offices of the
church. In the Lutheran church both can be ordained. In time
we will have both male and female bishops. No doubt the presiding bishop will be a woman some day. Perhaps men and women
do tend to have different abilities and gifts. That is still a complicated, unsolved question. But whatever abilities we men and
women have, let each of us use them as the Spirit wills, both
within the church and in our daily lives.

It is an exciting time to be a woman in the church. The opportunities for service on all levels are there, even to the point
of the church mandating itself to have 40–50% women represented on different levels of church government. It is now up to
us to become prepared, qualified, and active. After being a delegate to the 1986 Lutheran World Federation Assembly in Bu-
dapest, Hungary—another church organization setting itself a
goal of 40–50% participation by women—I received a publication
from the Women's Department of the Lutheran World Federation in which they begged for qualified women to step forward
and assume the positions that were open. At that point they had
found only a small fraction of the quota. Many opportunities are
there, waiting for us!

The same is true in all other areas: our national church office,
regional church offices, synodical church offices, local congregations, government offices, and many others. We need to become qualified. It is a new time for women today, a far cry from
what yesterday was, and this is only the beginning.

Am I a Lay Minister?

To come back to the point in my own life where these issues
are alive for me personally: As a nonordained but trained hospital

chaplain, am I a lay minister? Probably, but that term is so battered it may not be helpful.

Do I proclaim God's message? Surely. Read and share Scripture, give counsel, pray with others? Of course. All Christians do that in appropriate circumstances.

Do I administer the sacraments? On particular occasions I do, when a patient's own parish pastor is not available or the pressure of time and physical condition of the patient make waiting inadvisable. This is an area where individual circumstances vary and where Lutheran theology permits some latitude.

Should I become ordained? Would it make my work more effective? More valid? Some of my sisters are being ordained, some are not. Roman Catholic women are not permitted ordination, but they are doing superb work in the Christian church. The Lutheran church does not have a clear-cut answer about who should be ordained and who should not. But the first thing we need to do is clean up our vocabulary, so at least we can have some clarity in the discussion.

8

Whether Women, Too, Can Be Pastors

JANET LANDWEHR

When the editor of this book first asked me to write an essay on the biblical warrants for women's ordination, I almost refused. It's not that I think the topic trivial or irrelevant. Rather, I worry that by focusing on such an issue, we may delude ourselves into thinking that a well-reasoned academic argument for women's ordination will overcome all opposition. In my experience, that simply isn't true.

I was not in the first wave of women seminarians and pastors who had to bear the burden of educating their parishioners (and often other pastors) on the validity of women's ordination. By the time I entered the system, many of the people I met had already experienced worship led by an ordained woman. The first immediate questions these people had about women's ordination had already been answered. The responses I met were much more visceral reactions, quite resistant to logical argument.

Before publication, a group of women students saw the title of the draft of this chapter and were quite insulted (perhaps not recognizing the allusion to Luther's essay *Whether Soldiers, Too, Can Be Saved*). How dare I suggest that there was still any question on the issue of women's ordination? But indeed there still is a question for many people in our congregations, a question not of theological interpretation but of deep emotional discomfort. That is an issue to which I want to return at the end of this chapter.

But first we do need to look at the biblical bases for women's ordination, to build a firm foundation for future discussions. We may not be able to change the feelings and prejudices of others with logical argument, but at least we can maintain our own integrity by responsible study of God's Word.

The exploration of biblical authority for permitting or rejecting women's ordination raises many issues of biblical interpretation. A few assumptions are made for this chapter.

Development of doctrine.   The Bible is not a textbook in systematic theology, and therefore does not present a final and complete answer to all doctrinal questions. Even some of our most basic understandings, such as our theologies of Eucharist, the Holy Trinity, and the nature of Jesus Christ, were not completely spelled out in the biblical witness but were refined over centuries in the Christian church. We cannot, therefore, look to the Bible for a simple and obvious answer on whether women's ordination is *required, permitted,* or *prohibited.*

In this essay I will not attempt to prove that women's ordination is *required.* (Such a discussion would require extensive inquiry into concepts such as *justice* and *shalom.* Additionally, if one attempted to prove that women's ordination were required in the church, what implications would that have for the centuries of church history when women were not ordained?)

Rather, we will simply try to show that there is nothing in the Bible that *prohibits* women's ordination, and we will do that by looking at those passages cited most frequently by the opponents of women's ordination.

Consistency.   The Bible contains many different kinds of material which need to be interpreted in different ways, depending on their context and historical setting. However, for one type of material, and particularly within one book, we need to be consistent in our method of interpretation. It is simply silly to interpret one verse absolutely literally and then to dismiss the next verse as historically conditioned or allegorical.

Theological integrity.   The Bible does not consist of prooftexts which we may quote in snippets to argue a particular point. (If we try, the brighter of our opponents will merely respond with contradicting snippets. As Matt. 4:6 shows, even the devil can quote Scripture.) Rather, we must develop an overall understanding of God's message to us that is consistent with the entire biblical witness.

With these guidelines in mind, we will quickly survey five parts of Scripture: creation narratives; cultic laws; the life of Jesus; Pauline Epistles and Acts; and I Timothy. Additionally, we will look at two other theological arguments against women's ordination, based on allegory and on tradition.

Creation Narratives

Looking at the creation narratives in Genesis, we need to ask if we can find any inherent difference between men and women that would disqualify women from serving in the ordained ministry. Discussion usually revolves around three parts of the narratives.

Genesis 1:27a. Often the first half of this verse is quoted to imply that only men are created in God's image. But that interpretation is inconsistent with the second half of the verse: "Male and female [God] created them." Clearly, it is humanity that is created in God's image.

There are numerous suggestions as to just what the "image and likeness of God" is. However, the second half of the verse suggests that our sexuality has something to do with it! One interpretation of the *imago Dei* is the ability to have relationships of intimacy and ecstasy—intimacy and ecstasy which we have in our relationship with God, but which is also mirrored in our human sexual relationships.

Genesis 2:18-23. To understand this passage properly, we need to understand that "Adam" is not so much a personal name, nor a noun meaning "male human," as it is a noun meaning "earth creature," a being made out of the red clay earth (Hebrew: *adama*) into whom God has breathed his Spirit. This creature is not described as specifically male. The first indication of sexuality is when the creature's rib is used to form a woman, and *what remains* is a man.

The woman is said to be a helper fit for the man. This does not imply a subordinate status. Rather, the woman is indeed of the same nature as the man, and therefore fit for partnership with him in a way no human–animal pairing could ever be. The same Hebrew word (*ezer*) that describes woman as a helper for man is also the word used in the Psalms (30:10; 54:4) to describe God as our helper.

The woman is made from only a part of Adam. But, it needs to be noted that after this "operation" the remaining man is no longer the original whole "Adam-the-earth-creature" either. Both the man and the woman are incomplete in themselves, and it is only in their union that they achieve completeness.

This theme occurs also in the creation myths of ancient pagan cultures, but with a difference. In Greek myth, for instance, the complete and perfect original beings were split apart as punishment for angering the gods, and the incomplete halves, men and women, are doomed to search unsuccessfully forever for their missing halves. In the Bible, the splitting-apart is God's way of blessing his creatures with intimate companionship.

Certainly there are many unmarried people in our world who live fulfilled lives without being married, but even for those people, God's blessing is present in all the variety of other close, committed, and caring relationships. It is those relationships that make our lives distinctively human.

Gen. 3:16b. It is important to note where in the narratives this verse occurs. The statement "[Your husband] shall rule over you" is not part of the way in which humans were created, but rather is part of the punishment for their sinfulness. Male domination is not the way God intended us to be, but rather is punishment for human sin.

It has often been noted that women's liberation is actually men's liberation as well. Gender-role stereotypes keep men as well as women from experiencing the fullness of their humanity—both strength and gentleness, both emotion and rational thinking, both leadership and support. As our human lives become ever more redeemed by God's grace, we are increasingly freed from the burden of the domination/subordination punishment, and drawn ever closer to the order of creation in which men and women were blessed with partnership and true companionship.

In summary, the creation narratives properly interpreted cannot be used to prove the supposed inferiority of women.

Cultic Laws

There are numerous cultic laws in the Hebrew Scriptures having to do with women's subordination, and with their ritual uncleanness especially during menstruation and following childbirth (Lev. 12; Lev. 15:19ff). However, there are numerous other cultic laws in the Hebrew scriptures as well, and it is inconsistent to quote those dealing with women while ignoring the rest.

Very few Christians these days honor the cultic dietary laws ("keep kosher"). Even fewer know and keep the more obscure laws, such as the one (Lev. 19:19) that prohibits the use of two fibers in one article of clothing. (So much for cotton-polyester blends!)

This is as it should be. Christ has fulfilled the law for us (Matt. 5:17) and we are now justified apart from the law (Rom. 3:19-26). In a vision (Acts 10), Peter was taught that nothing God has made is unclean. Although this vision referred specifically to food, it is reasonable to assume that the natural God-created rhythms of women's bodies are not unclean either.

The Teachings and Actions of Jesus

Many scholars have commented on the favorable attitude Jesus had towards women in his life and teachings. There are numerous times he accepted women in ways unheard of for a respectable rabbi of his generation. In Jesus' time, most men would have considered the woman with the flow of blood (Luke 8:43-48) "unclean" according to ritual Jewish law. Most good Jewish men would never have taken a drink from the woman at the well (John

4:7-30), because she was both a woman and a Samaritan. Most self-respecting men would not have accepted the attentions of the "woman of the city" (a euphemism for prostitute) who anointed Jesus' feet (Luke 7:36-50). But in all these situations, Jesus received these women as the equal of any man.

Some critics stress that the twelve disciples were men. But these twelve were not the only followers of Jesus. Mary Magdalene, for instance, is mentioned with Jesus in each of a number of towns through which Jesus traveled, implying that she was traveling with him just as the disciples were. Although the Gospels do not mention women as being present at the Last Supper, neither do they exclude them. It is quite possible that women were present, and that the evangelists simply did not think them worthy of mention. (Someone, after all, must have prepared the food!)

At the resurrection, it is Mary Magdalene to whom the risen Christ first appeared. It is she who announced the good news to the other disciples (who, incidentally, didn't believe her [Luke 24:10-11] since in that time a woman's testimony was thought to be so unreliable that it was not even acceptable in courts of law). The early church honored Mary Magdalene as the "apostle to the apostles," a tradition lost in our church today.

The specific role of the disciples, the specific implications of the term "disciple," and even the identity of "the twelve" are not clearly stated with consistency in the Gospels. There did seem to be an inner circle of Jesus' male friends, it is true, but after Jesus' ascension, the ministry of the church was not limited just to these twelve. They were to commission others, and indeed some (such as Paul) were commissioned to the ministry without the intervention of "the twelve." The Gospels give evidence of the importance of women as well as men speaking as witnesses of the miraculous power of Jesus Christ (e.g., John 4:28-29).

The Epistles

The Epistles contain many different kinds of material, ranging from descriptions of the eschatological kingdom of God to instructions for day-to-day life in first century Palestine. To properly understand the Epistles, it helps to remember Luther's distinction between the two realms ("two kingdoms") in which we live simultaneously—the realm of God and the realm of humanity. The church is at once a manifestation of God's grace in the world and at the same time a human institution subject to sin.

In reading any part of the Epistles, we have to ask ourselves to what extent a particular passage is an enduring expression of God's grace and salvation, and to what extent it is a practical but culturally conditioned advice to a human institution of 1900 years ago.

1 Cor. 14:34.   Does this verse really forbid women to take leadership roles in worship? Most scholars understand this to refer not to preaching but to curious whispered questioning, especially since the next verse tells the women to wait until they get home to satisfy their curiosity.

This passage must be contrasted with 1 Cor. 11:5. Here Paul fusses about women keeping their heads covered while prophesying—but he apparently has no problem with properly attired women prophesying in the midst of the worshiping assembly.

1 Peter 3:7.   In this verse women are called the "weaker sex," but so what? "God chose what is weak in the world to shame the strong" (1 Cor. 1:27b), and "[God's] power is made perfect in weakness" (2 Cor. 12:9).

Husbands and wives.   Some frequently cited passages (1 Cor. 7:1-4, Eph. 5:21-33) have nothing at all to do with the general role of women in the leadership of the church, but rather with the specific relationship between husbands and wives.

First, it should be noted that these passages do not require "submission" of wives only, but corresponding submission of husbands to their wives as well (Eph. 5:21,25,28; 1 Cor. 7:4b).

Second, even if one accepts these historically conditioned household instructions as still relevant today, it is unwarranted to extrapolate these marital rules to general relationships between all men and all women.

Summary.   All the passages cited above are understood by many scholars as culturally conditioned rules for household behavior. In the more central passages of the Epistles that speak about our call to service in God's church (e.g., 1 Cor. 12), no limitations are placed on women's service. And in Gal. 3:27ff, our status before God is clearly not limited by our gender.

Finally, it should be noted that women (e.g., Chloe, Lydia, Nympha, Prisca) are mentioned often in Acts and the Epistles as leaders in their Christian communities and hosts of their communities' worship celebrations.

1 Timothy

The first letter to Timothy (which scholars do not consider authentically Pauline) presents the most clearly defined challenge to women's ordination in 1 Tim. 2:11-12 (women learn in silence; keep silent). But interpretation of this passage must be examined for consistency and theological integrity.

Consistency.   Any person claiming 1 Tim. 2:11-12 as a literal proof text should be expected to interpret 1 Tim. 3:2,12 similarly. As these verses demand that bishops and deacons be "husband of one wife," they would seem, if taken literally, to deny ordination to celibate deacons, priests, and bishops. Do they therefore deny the validity of the entire Western Church for centuries prior to the Reformation? Do they deny the validity of the Roman Catholic priesthood today?

Alternatively, if a person wishes to explain away 1 Tim. 3:2,12 as historically or contextually conditioned, then why cannot the same argument be used to explain 1 Tim. 2:11-12?

I think both of these passages are historically conditioned expressions of the need for the church to maintain as much societal respectability as is consistent with the proclamation of the gospel, so that no barriers of outrageous behavior (however that may be interpreted in the current century) will be placed in the way of the gospel. In today's world which accepts women in a full range of professional roles, the idea of women in the ministry, in my opinion, can no longer seriously be considered an obstacle to the proclamation of the gospel.

Theological integrity.   A person who wishes to claim a literal interpretation of 1 Tim. 2:11-12 (and of 1 Tim. 3:2,12) must still face several problems. The first occurs in the very next verses (2:13-15), which present a strained interpretation of the creation narratives. (Gen. 3:17-19 condemns Adam equally with Eve.)

Also, how are passages like Gal. 3:28 (neither male nor female; all one in Christ Jesus) to be explained? And what about the times when women witnessed to men about Jesus in the Gospels (e.g. John 4:28-30; John 20:18)?

There are some branches of conservative Christian theology which do attempt to reconcile a literal interpretation of 1 Timothy with these other passages. But such theologies usually achieve that reconciliation by putting heavy emphasis on legalism, judgment, and condemnation, and by downplaying God's grace, forgiveness, and redemption. In doing so, that theology matches neither my study of the Bible nor my experience of God's gracious love.

Argument by Allegory

Some of the recurring arguments against women's ordination are based on allegory. Many of these arguments are exceedingly weak and would not be worth mentioning except for the frequency of their recurrence.

Alter Christus. The most common argument is that the priest is to represent Christ and therefore must resemble Christ. We must note that, properly understood, Lutherans do accept the priest (or pastor) as *re*-presenting Christ—in the sense that the pastor is a means through which Christ is made again present in our midst, through the power of the Holy Spirit. But that does not equate the person of the pastor with the person of Christ.

In what ways must the priest resemble Christ? Some would argue that a female cannot represent the male Jesus. But few people expect priests to have other physical similarities to Jesus Christ—such as height, weight, hair color, eye color, or skin color. (And, as the snide comment goes, very few Christian priests these days are Middle Eastern Jews born of virgins.) The argument becomes nothing but prejudice.

The Bridegroom.   Some would cite Eph. 5, and suggest that as Christ is to be the head of the church universal, the bridegroom of the church his bride, the priest is also to be the surrogate head of the local congregation and its bridegroom. But this is a misunderstanding of the ministry, at least in our Lutheran understanding. We teach that the ordained ministry is one among many equally valuable forms of service. The priest is one of many members of the body of Christ, not its surrogate head.

Tradition

The role of tradition must be taken seriously in any theological argument. Our understanding of God's will grows slowly over time, shaped by the power of the Holy Spirit, and clearly that understanding has for many centuries not included the ordination of women.

However, the Holy Spirit leads us to grow in new understandings. The Lutheran church was born from Spirit-led growth in theology and continues, according to Luther, to stand in need of continual reformation. Change in our tradition must never be made lightly, or merely for the sake of keeping up with current fashion. But deliberate and prayerful change can be seen as the continuing work among us of our living and all-powerful God. A change such as the acceptance of the ordination of women is not a change to be taken lightly, but it is a serious and appropriate step that the Lutheran church has taken in its continuing growth led by the Spirit and faithful to its Creator.

Personal Reflection

This returns us to my opening concern. In my experience, I have found that all the facts and theological arguments in the world on the subject of women's ordination change the minds of only a few people. There are many, both men and women, who come to this discussion having already made a decision against the equality of women. These days, such people rarely attempt a logical explanation of their prejudices; rather, they simply state them.

In one parish, during a time when I had sole pastoral responsibility, a woman lay leader informed me that the parish would henceforth have a guest preacher once a month. Since the people of the parish considered preaching one of my greatest strengths, I was quite suspicious of this decision. After a bit of discussion in which various red herrings were suggested (variety in preaching styles, "to give me a break," and so forth), she finally admitted that "some people in the parish want to see a man in the pulpit at least once a month." There was no logical rationale offered for this statement; it was unabashedly presented as simple prejudice.

In a profession like ministry which is so reliant on good relations with one's parishioners and on friendly persuasion, how is one supposed to address ingrained prejudice? Those women who do not capitulate to prejudice are often seen as "troublemakers" or "unable to get along." This is a problem that can be solved neither by scholarly debate nor by righteous resistance. We need to address ingrained prejudice against women by digging to its roots.

Many people have very limited understandings of their own gender roles. A man might understand his masculinity to require his being masterful, providing leadership, and therefore he may feel threatened when a woman takes that role of leadership and asks the man to be the follower. A woman might see herself as in need of protection and therefore feel denied and threatened by another women who does not gain protection by submissiveness. A woman might think her role requires her to focus on private family matters and therefore she is confused by another woman who works primarily in the public sphere. The opposition of these people to women's ordination is a manifestation of this limited self-understanding and the fears of perceived threats caused by such limitations.

Any attempt to change the "symptom" of opposition to women's ordination through rational theological argument is quite likely to fail, because the underlying problem is not one of intellectual misunderstanding but one of personal insecurity.

The most important use of the information in this chapter, then, is to support those women and men who recognize that the gospel offers empowerment. We need to be able to counter arguments from "experts" who try to misuse the Bible to subjugate other people. Our reasoned arguments are unlikely to change the minds of those fearful people who already firmly oppose women's ordination, but they may win over those whose minds are not yet set against equality.

More importantly, though, we need to continue to work towards *shalom*, towards a growing understanding of wholeness for us all. We as a society need to learn that both men and women need all the God-given dimensions of our lives—leading and following; thinking and caring; being independent and being interdependent; having private relationships and public relationships. Only to the extent that we accept our own wholeness and acknowledge the wholeness of our sisters and brothers will we be able to accept the fact that ordained ministers are called forth from the whole people of God.

9

The Call to Ministry
of Word and Sacrament

JANE STROHL

The Certainty

A seminary received a letter from a former student, a disgruntled ex-candidate for the ministry who was dismissed because of inadequate academic performance. No one professor was responsible for the decision; all faculty members had a hand in the judgments that brought about academic probation and ultimately, dismissal. Their decision was sound, but it produced distressing effects.

For the student, convinced of a call from God and thereby qualified for the ordained ministry of the church, it was a tragedy. The student challenged the church which, through the seminary, seemed to be thwarting the will of the one who calls people to ministry. With unshaken self-assurance, the student told the faculty that (1) the call of God is more important than the call of the church, (2) wisdom is more important than knowledge, and (3) walking in faith is more important than standing in our beliefs.

I am prone to agree that wisdom is more important than knowledge, but I question the implied claim that one can be both wise and ignorant. A pastor who, like a skillful physician, is to apply the law and the gospel to the end that the fever of arrogant sin

113

might be broken and the stricken conscience might be strengthened and consoled, needs wisdom to assess the needs of those entrusted to her pastoral care, to know which word to speak when. Without knowledge of Scripture, church history and theology, she won't know what those words are, less how they can be misused as well as truly proclaimed.

As to the last claim about walking in faith being more important than standing in our beliefs, I admit some uncertainty as to its meaning. Is it possible to be in faith, that is, in a relationship of repentance, trust, obedience, and gratitude with the God who raised our Lord Jesus Christ from the dead, without holding some very specific convictions about this God's nature and activity and about the human condition? Christians believe that we are part of God's good creation yet sinful and unclean, Jesus Christ is indeed risen from the dead, and the one who made us is the same one who wrought this miracle for us and for our salvation. Is it possible to walk in faith without being able to conceptualize, articulate, and confess those things which we say norm our walking?

It is the student's first claim, however, that troubles me most of all. Is the call of God more important than the call of the church? Indeed, how do the two relate? For those of us charged with the responsibility of deciding whether the church should or should not issue a call to specific candidates for ministry as well as for those whose careers are subject to our determinations, this is an issue upon which we must be clear from the outset of our common endeavor.

The Blessing of Community

Community is one of the greatest blessings and also a troublesome burden. As much as we would like to be joined to one another, we often find it easier to go our independent ways and prefer to hold what we hold most dear most privately. Our faith is a glaring example of this, and it seems to me that God, in establishing the church, has made it clear that hard as it is to live together, we are formed to be a holy people, not a collection of individuals to whom the Lord only relates one-on-one.

The means of grace are given to the church. Baptism makes one a member of the communion of saints, bound before God to St. Teresa of Avila and to the present Bishop of Rome, as well as to the Sunday school superintendent in one's local congregation. The Eucharist, in which our High Priest knits us into the body of Christ and offers us to the one he called Father, is open to all who confess Christ's name and is thus a public proclamation among the faithful. It would be wrong for any one believer to transform her privilege to eat and drink into the right to appropriate the supper for her own ends, to celebrate it at her kitchen table with a few select friends instead of joining in the public celebration with believers known and unknown, with persons cherished as well as with those who try her patience. It is an essential part of the grace conveyed by the sacrament that in those moments our separations are overcome, so that with one voice and action, before God and the world, we may confess the Lord's death until he comes.

This communal aspect is crucial too in our understanding of the ministry. The office of Word and Sacrament, like Baptism and the Lord's Supper, is given to the church. The call to take up this office comes from God, but Lutheran theology insists that it is mediated through the community. I have had numerous students, as they seek to sort out the promptings of their own hearts, ask me how I knew that I was called, and I answer, "I knew I was called the day the Examining Panel of the Maryland Synod of the Lutheran Church in America voted to approve me for ordination."

To be honest, I was not always happy with the church's interventions during my seminary career. I had the feeling sometimes that these people were telling me they knew my mind better than I knew it myself. I didn't always agree with their decisions as to the fitness or lack thereof of my classmates. I even questioned their judgment as to the appointments they made to such sensitive decision-making bodies as the Church Vocations Committee and the Examining Panel. Now that I'm on the other side of the process, I'm still uneasy. As seriously as we representatives of the church take our responsibility, as much as we pray for the Spirit's guidance in our deliberations, we undoubtedly do make some mistakes for which other people will pay the price: either disappointed seminarians or poorly served parishioners and their inadequate pastors.

I think this is a particularly troubling issue for women because the church's attitude toward us has been so discriminatory. People have asked me how long I knew I wanted to be a pastor before I went to seminary. Did I cherish the hope in my heart from childhood on like some of my male colleagues profess to have done? The answer is no. I was no visionary; I imagined my future in terms of the possibilities I saw around me.

When the church which now counts me on its clerical rolls was busy debating the ordination of women, I was a high school student, worrying about the length of my English term paper and the uncertainty of being asked to the senior prom. I went off to college with thoughts of becoming a translator at the United Nations or a literature professor. I don't remember hearing anything in my home congregation about the historic vote at the national convention to ordain women. Moreover, even after the experiences of the ensuing four years left me with the bedrock conviction that I would seek work in the church, I didn't consider ordained ministry. I had never seen it done by a woman, and in my search for employment with the church, it was never suggested to me. (I might add that not all the women pastors of my vintage were so unimaginative in their youth. One seminary classmate told me that as a little girl she used to play Communion with friends, celebrating her make-believe sacrament with hosts cut out of toilet paper. What an impression those communion wafers must have made on her! Another friend told me that she harassed her confirmation pastor with questions as to why women couldn't be ordained. In exasperation he finally cut off the discussion with the remark, "They just aren't.")

As I look back on my own history, I wonder if the limited possibilities presented to me didn't confuse my sense of calling. I was committed, determined to take whatever opportunity the church saw fit to offer me, and my ardor outstripped my judgment. I accepted a position to go to Japan as an English teacher, but in the course of my training with other missionaries preparing to travel to various overseas assignments, it became clear to me that I was ill-equipped for the job. Suddenly I saw myself as a well-intentioned young woman on a spiritual high, who had either the naiveté or the audacity to think that would be enough to carry her through as a messenger of the gospel in a foreign culture of which she knew nothing and, to be honest, in which she had not up to that time been particularly interested. Mortified and defeated, I withdrew from the program and went home.

I got a job in Washington, D.C., and spent much time in the succeeding months trying to figure out what that fiasco had to say about my sense of calling. Not only had I not kept my hand on the plow, I had actually turned tail and fled back across the field. I really didn't know whether I could expect to have a second chance in the church. Then my brother Ralph, who was a second-year student at Gettysburg Seminary at the time, helped me get back on track. He convinced me that my withdrawal from the Japan program had been prudent rather than cowardly, that it was all right to have questions about the Christian faith and uncertainty about where one's calling should lead. I hadn't wronged God by faltering, but I would wrong both the Lord and myself, said Ralph, if I didn't pursue those questions and explore my sense of vocation. He suggested seminary as the ideal place to undertake that quest. I replied, "You mean maybe become a pastor?" He pointed out that women did that sort of thing these days, and I poured forth all my objections as to how people wouldn't readily accept women in the pulpit and how I didn't know whether I could take the pressure and the aggravation. Ralph asked me if I was unable to see myself in such a position, and I realized quite clearly there and then that I had no difficulty with that possibility. Then he cautioned me not to make other people's problems mine. If I was at peace with the idea, I should get on with it. I was, and I did, and my brother's loving advice has kept me steady at many a disconcerting moment in my career.

As you can see, I took a long way around to get where I needed
to be, and the church, particularly as I encountered it at Gettysburg Seminary, did much to help me find my place. But I
often mourn the Lutheran women before me, whose sense of
calling took them awandering but whose church didn't allow
them to come out where they belonged. In 1970 the ordination
of women proved to be an idea whose time had come for the
majority of American Lutherans, but its arrival was not timely
enough for some women.

For the reasons given above, I, unlike the disgruntled student
of my opening paragraphs, am not prepared to overthrow the
church's prerogatives in the process of selecting and authorizing
those who hold the office of the ministry. I am not willing to let
one individual's assurance that he or she has a call from God be
enough. That call, like all inspirations purportedly from the Spirit, must be tested. Yet the experience of women has revealed this
process to be untrustworthy at times. The insidious element of
sexism threatens to undermine the force of ecclesiastical judgments for their female hearers.

It is hard to discern substantive factors which speak against
one's candidacy for ordination when one suspects that the objections are a mere smokescreen. Because the issue often is one's
femaleness, it is easy to imagine this to be the prime mover in
every decision, even a favorable one. Women who have (so to
speak) succeeded, whose calling the church has confirmed and
whose careers the powers that be have advanced, may well wonder
what lies behind their support. Is this predominantly male institution really trying to change itself, to be open to the participation of women to the degree that its structure may be profoundly affected? Or are a few women taken up here and there
to give credibility to a *status quo* that has no intention of relaxing
its grip on power? Many of us have days when we can't help but
ask the question, "Am I taken seriously?" Despite the ordination
certificate on the wall and the bishop's assurance that the pros-
pects for a second call are good, the doubt is never wholly laid
to rest.

We look around and see a liberal sprinkling of women pastors in our parishes and of women ministers in the agencies of the church. We even find a few women on the seminary faculties. It's a sight that cheers and encourages me. Yet in my darker moments I compare us to the parsley garnishing a sandwich platter; it makes the sandwiches look better but very few people bother to taste it and benefit from the sprig's healthy effects. It grieves me that it is so easy to project this kind of insecurity indiscriminately and thus to poison one's calling and one's relationship with so many good and faithful people in the church.

Part of the responsibility of hearing and answering the call to ordained ministry in this generation is to contend with these ambiguities. The means of grace are given to the Christian community and to know God's love we must find and occupy our place among our brothers and sisters in Christ. This means taking the chance of being hurt and even mistreated. It means taking the challenge of reforming that community and helping it to learn anew the lessons of justice and love of the neighbor. It is worth remembering the caveat a friend once gave me as I waxed paranoid about my status in the church. She cautioned me against looking for slights and potential enemies and using them as instruments to diminish my calling and ability. It is hard enough to fathom one's own heart without trying to guess the motivations of others, she said. She figured that whatever the reasons that lay behind a particular position becoming available to her, the job was now hers, and so she would gladly seize the opportunity to exercise her ministry and, with God's help, make the most of it.

The Grace of Perseverance

I have no hard statistics before me, but I have the impression that women clergy are leaving the ministry in disturbing numbers. Each time I read the roster changes in *The Lutheran* I wonder what story lies behind the simple statement that a woman has gone on leave from call. The women seminarians returning from

internship have expressed their concern over the number of dis-
heartened women clergy they have met out in parishes. They are
seeking to take some preventive measures in their senior year so
that they will not burn out prematurely. It terrifies them to think
that having made it through seminary and landed that first call,
the worst may be yet to come.

When I had been ordained just over seven years, I confess I
endured a bout of vocational seven-year-itch right on schedule.
After an arduous stint in graduate school I was finally on to my
second call, and as I fumbled along, I wondered if what had
carried me so far had been at heart deluded ambition rather than
a true vocation. My ministry had been nurtured and exercised
exclusively on the Atlantic coast. Now I was transported to a
place utterly unfamiliar, a place where I had no personal connections and no church ties. Leaving one's past behind can be
liberating, but it can also be oppressive. I took stock of all I felt
I had cut out of my world or left behind for the sake of my career,
and my life seemed as narrow as the grave. Too long under the
thrall of Mother Church and Father Academia, I thought; time
to get out and recover a broader horizon and that sense of evangelical joy I never thought would waver. When I wasn't energized
by the prospect of rebellion, I was crippled by guilt. Just like
my abortive mission to Japan, here I was standing on the brink
of failing my Lord again. And I tormented myself with the
thought that if I abandoned my vocation, I would simultaneously
expel myself from a state of grace.

I will not make so bold as to claim that every pastor goes
through crises like this, but I will declare that I am not a rarity.
As Luther counseled the troubled souls in his care, you must
combat such temptation with spiritual weapons. One of the most
powerful of these is the companionship and comfort fellow Christians can provide. When we falter in our commitment, other
people can tide us over with their strength. By acknowledging
the problem and articulating it, we can begin to deal with it rather
than allowing it to swell out of all proportion in solitude.

The Christian servant ethic can be perverted into the idea that
any and every sacrifice is worth making. We are indeed called to

take up our crosses and follow Christ, but as Luther pointed out time and time again, it is neither necessary nor pleasing to God that we seek our own crosses. Ministry, not to mention life, will be difficult enough without stacking the deck heavily in favor of pain right from the outset. The Spirit may well carry one to unforeseen and even uninviting situations. I do not mean that one should give one's own needs and desires absolute priority so that we act, as Joseph Sittler described it, as if we were demanding, "Listen Lord, thy servant speaketh" (*Gravity and Grace,* Augsburg [1986], p. 58).

On the other hand, I can't help but think of a friend of mine who found herself falling into the dangerous habit of only paying pastoral calls to those parishioners who were guaranteed to criticize and complain and make her feel wretched. She made a conscious effort to include in her daily rounds visits to contented, enthusiastic families and to cultivate relationships with members who talked to her about deeper questions and broader concerns than the dearth of youth group advisors or the need for repairs to the sound system. It took her a while to convince herself that the fact that she had fun, that some visits actually could release her for a bit from the pressure of parish duties, did not mean that they weren't part of doing her job. Similarly, I think one can honor one's commitments to Christ and his church and still satisfy desires that one feels are essential to one's well-being.

Perhaps one of the root causes of the exodus of women clergy from the ministry is their hesitance to make these claims for themselves. Calls are so often hard to come by, and we question whether it is appropriate or wise to say no when the bishop and a congregation present us with an opportunity. Such a dilemma is never easily resolved, but one should be motivated by knowledge of oneself at least as much as by concern for the political realities of the call process.

Moreover, I suspect that when women pastors find themselves in unhappy ministries, they tend to lose heart and give up. Ministry is an art cultivated over a lifetime, and one's progress in it is never consistently straightforward. Our educational system has

accustomed us to measuring accomplishment in four-year seg-
ments; after 48 months one sees tangible fruits and receives ob-
jective affirmation of one's efforts. It is not so with the parish.
My best friend from seminary and I had a wonderful conversation
at the end of our seventh year on the clergy roster. She sang me
the praises of patience, pointing out that I was too quick to jump
to the conclusion when the going got tough that I was in the
wrong place. Although she has been receiving strong encourage-
ment to look for a third call that would bring her back to her
home state, she admitted to me that while she longs to be closer
to her family, she realizes that she's not yet ready to move. The
first year or so in her present congregation was marred by conflict
and unkindness, but pastor and people have ridden out the
storms. This is a community that has struggled and learned the
gracious lessons of forgiveness and reconciliation and increased
in its power to love. Now after almost six years she is beginning
to feel secure in her work, able to branch out a bit, to do new
things, and to savor the fruits of the ministry in that place.

The Word of God will not return to its source empty. The
harvest will be bountiful, and we women workers in the Lord's
vineyard need not despair of our ministries just because it's a
long growing season.

10
In a Different Voice

STEPHANIE FREY

W hen I look out over the congregation while leading the
liturgy on Sunday morning, one of the faces I see most
clearly is that of six-year-old Anne. She is standing in the
pew, right on the aisle alongside of her parents and brothers. An
able reader now in her first-grade year, she holds her *Lutheran
Book of Worship* high, following along in the liturgy she has
known by heart for several years. She sings her heart out, and
sometimes looks up at me with a broad smile. Behind her, as I
look further down the long aisle, I see my own reflection in the
windows at the back of the sanctuary—making the sign of the
cross, raising my hands for prayer, extending them for the greeting and the peace. Seeing Anne and my own reflection behind
her reminds me that for her the body of Christ is being reflected
in a new way and in a different voice. This is true not only for
Anne, but for the whole congregation here and in all the other
places where women clergy are now presiding and preaching at
worship. Anne and many other children will grow up thinking
a new way. Those children whose baptismal certificates are signed
by a woman will surely be a new generation in whom this "new
thing" that has come into being will no longer be new, but ordinary in the best sense of the word.

Anne's mother tells me that on Sunday afternoons Anne often
puts on a robe of some sort, ties a "cincture" around her waist,

and proceeds to lead and sing the liturgy on her own, to a congregation of dolls and bears and occasionally her own brothers. The liturgy has lifted off the printed page and lives inside of Anne. She is "ritually competent." In other words, the liturgy is not flat for her. It has a shape and she can sing it and do it herself. She may not cognitively understand all the dimensions of the words yet, but surely it has a certain meaning. It is where she belongs, where she feels at home. It has taken on a life of its own.

The culture in which we live is a highly ritualized one, but in new ways. I have the sense that people are observers, now more than ever, in our increasingly high-tech way of life. People watch sporting events religiously via television if not in person. The chants of the crowd at those occasions form the liturgy, the "people's work." The possibility of worshiping at home in front of the TV because of the surplus of video evangelists has become the church for many folk who have some reason for not getting out to their congregation come Sunday morning. Ritual in the society has taken on a new look. It certainly shapes life for individuals, but creates a passivity in the participants, making them observers more than the makers or doers of liturgy.

Ritual shapes our days from waking to bedtime, whether it be the rituals of showering and toothbrushing to prepare ourselves for the day, or our patterns of eating, or the traditions of "hello and good-bye" in the homes and family groupings in which we live and work. It has often been the case over the centuries that women have been the ones primarily responsible for transmitting ritual in families. When mothers are the parents who have primary responsibilities for childrearing, they do the fundamental skillteaching to little ones who must learn to do certain things even before they understand the rationale behind them. Children are fed and taught to eat long before they are taught about nutrition or the digestive system. Much of that learning comes by way of imitation and mimicry, but it shapes our lives.

In much the same way the liturgy of the church in corporate worship is ritual. It is repetitive, but rich in meaning, and comes to live in our hearts. When that happens, the "people's work" of liturgy makes us active participants in worship and not just observers who watch a pastor do it for us. All of us as God's people invoke the presence of God when we come together for worship. In Psalm 34 the psalmist invites us: "O magnify the Lord with me." As we join in the liturgy of the whole faith community, and our many voices become a common voice of praise and prayer, God is enlarged for us in a way far different from what happens in private devotion and prayer.

When we of the congregation all sing the Kyrie, "Lord, have mercy," we ask God's peace in all the word, in all the church, and in the "holy house" in which we worship. Our sense of God's work and God's presence expands in the words of our mutual prayer. When we all sing, "This is the feast of victory for our God! Alleluia!" we are granted a vision of a banqueting table that extends to seat all of God's people. That vision is enhanced by watching our brothers and sisters in faith move toward the Lord's table for a "foretaste of the feast to come." Our sense of God's presence is enlarged in that communal, or corporate, setting in a way that cannot happen for the individual alone. And when we pray for the "whole people of God in Christ Jesus, and for all people according to their needs," we lay claim to a God whose loving arms span the globe and whose ears hear our pleas and petitions with a greatness far beyond our knowing.

In all of that, the liturgy heals and enlivens us as we gather in the sanctuary week by week for a time to rest in God's Word and to be fed at the table. The liturgy challenges us and sends us out again to our respective callings in the community and world. When seminary classmates of mine spent well over a year waiting for call, and time was heavy on their hands, they remarked that sometimes it was only the very act of singing the liturgy in the middle of a congregation that provided healing and strength through the long wait. The post-Communion prayer that says, "We give you thanks, Almighty God, for the healing power of this gift of life . . ." takes on new depth at such times.

As a woman who presides at worship, I find that a good deal of the life-shaping ritual taught to me by my mother and father is also part of the liturgical setting and worship. Hospitality is very much a part of leading worship. A good deal has been written about that of late. It ought not be thought of as a uniquely feminine contribution to congregational worship, and yet as women we are trained by our parents and the culture to attend to matters of hospitality—the welcoming of people, the courtesy of listening carefully to their concerns and needs, the setting of the family table, the serving of the family meal, the washing of children. In preparing for each Sunday I discover my own attentiveness to the details of worship hospitality in the readying of the sanctuary and the preparation of the sacraments. The sense of the family arriving when people begin to assemble for worship is strong, and as worship leaders we have a responsibility to welcome them with graciousness and warmth. If the Lord's table is indeed a "welcome table," then it behooves pastors and others in leadership to see to it that all good manners prevail for welcoming the congregational family to its home. As we increasingly see the need for congregations to nurture many members whose religious backgrounds and connections may be thin, or whose family situations are such that the church may provide them their only chance of really being at home, we cannot afford sloppiness in worship preparation.

Serving the Word: Preaching and Proclaiming

Serving the Word by preaching the gospel and administering the sacraments is at the heart of Lutheran worship. Article V of the *Augsburg Confession* makes it clear how those two events constitute the office of ministry:

> To obtain such faith God instituted the office of the ministry, that is, provided the Gospel and the sacraments. Through these, as through means, he gives the Holy Spirit, who works faith, when and where he pleases, in those who hear the Gospel. And the Gospel teaches that we have a gracious God, not by our own merits but by the merit of Christ, when we believe this.
>
> Condemned are the Anabaptists and others who teach that the Holy Spirit comes to us through our own preparations, thoughts,

and works without the external word of the Gospel. (*Book of Con-cord*, Fortress [1959], p. 31).

Article V is emphatic in saying that the source of ministry does not reside in the person, but rather in the gospel and sacraments themselves. That is a marvelous word for women and men alike. It is a freeing tradition in which to work because we all are "simul justus et peccator." We are justified saint and sinner at one and the same time. The ministry to which we are given is not de-pendent on our own merits, our good behavior or personal charm, or on our physical resemblance to Jesus Christ. To the old self in us who struggles valiantly to do and be everything in the congregations we serve, this is a word of freedom that can only come to us from outside ourselves.

The understanding of ministry as defined in Article V is freeing in another way as well. It is a definition that trusts the ongoing work of the Holy Spirit in the world, knowing that the Spirit will continue to reveal God and Christ to us in new ways. One of those ways is the movement within some church bodies over the last century, and for many Lutherans in the last quarter century, to ordain women, granting them the public ministry of preaching and presiding. The body of Christ to which all baptized people belong is now allowed to sing its gospel song in a new and fuller way. Because of the ordination of women, another set of experiences and perspectives is brought to bear in all the tasks of ministry.

The road is still long and hard for this movement, especially in the communions which look to apostolic succession and the matter of resemblance to Jesus Christ. The road may still be long and hard even within those churches that have granted ordina-tion. Not everyone holds the view of the parishioner who told me he didn't understand "why it should take anyone longer than 20 minutes to get used to a woman preacher." His vision of the church and its ministry was broad in scope. He was aware of Article V, knowing that the ministerial office has nothing to do with gender, and was genuinely impatient with those who were skeptical of the whole business of women's ordination. While I cherish that sort of support, I also know that for some the different voice, shape, and manner of a woman pastor is fearful and troubling. In most instances, familiarity and experience dissolve fear for the reluctant ones. But there are and will continue to be, I suspect, painful times for women clergy who come up against "the force of tradition" (Brita Stendahl, *The Force of Tradition*, Fortress, 1985).

In considering the role and experience of women as preachers and presiders, it is difficult to discern what is unique about the preaching done by women. When looking at biblical accounts of the witness of women, particularly in the story of the woman at the well, or in the Easter morning accounts of the women taking the news of the empty tomb back to the waiting disciples, the content of their witness does not seem different from the witness of a man. Yet in that day, when women's testimony was thought unreliable, their story was perceived and received differently precisely because they were women. Perhaps even today, the difference lies not so much in specific content, but in the matter of reception. That is where the different voice speaks loudly.

As I talk with people about their responses to hearing women preach, there are several themes that recur in their remarks: "She paints a picture when she preaches; I can always see what she is saying," or "She chooses one image or metaphor and stays with it throughout the sermon," or, in regard to funeral preaching, "She seemed to be able to describe the person so accurately, that he was made 'alive' to us again." When a woman preaches in this manner, the sermon's intimacy, its search for the telling sign, the key to the hearers' hearts and minds may be understood (by the hearers) as the unique gifts of women. It seems more true, however, to say that those are qualities which we have called "feminine" rather than being exclusively female attributes. Those are qualities which are part of good preaching, whatever the gender of the preacher. To the hearer, however, these words are perhaps *received* differently from the mouth of a woman than from a man.

One of my male colleagues in ministry and I were talking together about the matter of authority in preaching, and how men or women preachers may be perceived differently by their hearers. As we reflected on these dynamics that are really beyond our control, he remarked, "Sometimes I've wondered whether there is a danger for me, and maybe for other men, that the authority of our preaching could lie not in the Word itself, but in our own deep voices, or the loud and powerful delivery of a sermon—our male presence—with all the tradition that represents. It makes me wonder if women don't have a unique opportunity to let their authority be truly the authority of the Word, and not of the 'stage.' "

That poses an intriguing question as we think about the "different voice" women bring to the public ministry of preaching. It would be foolish to say that all men have deep voices and a loud or powerful style of preaching. It would also be foolish to say that all women preachers have soft voices and a quiet manner. But is there a way that the tradition of male preachers might have been granted an authority that has more to do with male presence than with the gospel? Knowing how strongly Luther stressed that the authority of the office and of the Word lies outside of ourselves, what might we be able to learn from the "new thing" of women preachers—from their style, their female presence, their different voice? Does the authority of the Word, the preaching of the power of God for salvation take on any new dimension for us as hearers when it comes from a woman's mouth?

It may also be that the life experience of women does play a part in the preaching they do. One parishioner made the remark, "I appreciate hearing the gospel preached through stories that aren't about athletics, team spirit, or the military." She *heard* the sermons of women differently because they were authentic to the preacher in a way which she could readily identify. The life experience women bring to preaching helps magnify God by bringing to life other scriptural images of God, or by seeing a Bible story from another perspective altogether. These are not better or worse than what is authentic for a man, simply different and worthy on their own account. When a pastor friend celebrated Advent during the final weeks of her first pregnancy, she became her own "visual aid," Sunday by Sunday, as she stood to preach. I have no doubt that the people she serves waited through Advent in a new way that year, full of eagerness not only for the baby to be born to their pastor and her husband, but also eager for the birth of Christ in their hearts new and fresh that Christmas. Pregnancy and birth is surely the one outstanding exception to the life experiences women and men have in common, and yet it may help us to think about the different voice women bring to the ministry of Word and Sacrament.

The Word to Be Preached

What shall we say of all this? Our speculative questions, our tentative wonderings about how things are different for the church and God's people given the ordination of women, our concern to be able to articulate the differences and commonalities in the experience of women and men, and the effect these things have on preaching are vitally important conversations in the church today. And yet, beyond all of that, we are called to recognize just what Article V of the *Augsburg Confession* recognizes: that it is still God's Word that gives power to any preaching, whether it is done by men or women. It is still the gifts of gospel and sacraments that bring us the "creative and redeeming Word" (*LBW*, p. 124), a resurrection word of life and healing and hope that we are privileged to proclaim.

When God spoke that first creative Word over the misty waters of chaos, before all time began, whole worlds were brought into being: suns and stars were hung in the heavens, the waters churned with the great creatures of the sea, green things brought life and color to the dry land. On the sixth day another creative Word was spoken, and male and female creatures were created, both in God's image.

The creative Word of God continues to be spoken among us in "many and various ways" (Heb. 1:1) but now is spoken to us most resoundingly in the Word that became flesh, Jesus Christ. Jesus went to the cross, speaking even there a word of forgiving grace to those who had lifted him on that awful tree. He went to the grave that could not hold him for long, and burst from it to declare victory over our last enemy, promising us a future out of what had appeared to be the darkest of all hours, the end of all things. That is the Word we are called to preach. That is the Word that frees us—men and women alike—to be about ministry in Christ's church. We are living in the grace of God, the ongoing Word of God. We are led to trust that even earthen vessels— weak and bumbling, arrogant and self-seeking, stiffnecked and stubborn though we are—can be used by God through the power of the gospel to be at work in the kingdom already present, and to hope with all our hearts and energy for the kingdom that is yet to be.

For those of us called by God's foolish wisdom to be preachers, there is always this word of resurrection to preach. "We do not preach *about* the resurrection week after week, but we *do* res- urrection preaching by which the life of the risen Christ is made accessible to those who are dying in sin and despair" (Richard Lischer, *A Theology of Preaching*, Abingdon [1981], p. 45, italics added).

To the people of God who wait and watch and hope, there is no other word to be spoken. The gospel of the risen Jesus is healing to those who are wounded by shattered relationships, or the pain of losing the land that was dear to them, or the agony of loneliness. It is hope for those who wait for a day when God's freedom will replace this world's bonds of oppression. It is com- fort for the lost and weak, a prod to the comfortable, and good news to all of us who sit in darkness.

Two prayers from the Vespers service in the *Lutheran Book of Worship* point us to our present task, and remind us of the walk into the future. It is always our task in preaching, as the first prayer states, to see to it that "God's Word may not be bound but have free course" (*LBW* Prayer 250)—the free course of the Spirit at work, continuing to give vision to us who are the church. In the second prayer we pray:

Lord God, you have called your servants to ventures of which we cannot see the ending, by paths as yet untrodden, through perils unknown. Give us faith to go out with good courage, not knowing where we go, but only that your hand is leading us and your love supporting us; through Jesus Christ our Lord. (*LBW* Prayer 251)

The way is uncharted, to be sure. But we are also seeing the fruits of a new day in the church as a more complete image of the body of Christ is represented in preaching and presiding, and in the life of worship for God's people. I am convinced that it is a gift of the Spirit for our time, in order to give yet another voice to the amazing word of resurrection that is ours in Jesus Christ. It is a different voice, but the same Lord, and the same calling. It is a different voice, but one that longs, too, to give witness to the resurrection. It is a different voice, but one that I hope will become ordinary, in the best sense of the word.

11

Pastor Married to Pastor

NORENE SMITH

PAUL OVERVOLD

Consider this list of occupations: doctor, astronaut, poet, lawyer, mail carrier, painter, movie star, teacher, electrician, business person, clergy couple . . .

Of all the vocations we considered as children, few if any of us considered "clergy couple" as an option. In the American Lutheran Church (ALC) at least, it wasn't even a possibility until 1970 and the advent of the ordination of women. Neither of us grew up imagining that we would someday become a member of this genre of "a pastor who is married to a pastor."

Our story began when, before meeting each other, we were led to seminary study to pursue our calls to the ordained ministry. After meeting, courtship, and marriage, we initially resisted the idea of both becoming pastors. Since Paul had already finished seminary and Norene was just beginning, she decided to quit and enter another field. That idea lasted about six months, until she decided that she wanted to finish seminary and we both trusted that we could figure out a way for it to work. At that time, in 1978, there were few clergy couples in the ALC, and our general sense was that they were considered "problems" and "difficult to place." How quickly times have changed in only nine years! A few weeks ago, Paul received a call from a District

Minister of another ALC district who wondered if we were interested in a new call. "Congregations are asking for clergy couples," he said.

In 1987, there were seven clergy couples in the 266 congregations of the Southwest Minnesota District of the ALC where we served. In the entire ALC, there were 84. While definitely a small percentage of the total clergy roster, clergy couples are making some important differences in the life of the church. In this article, we would like to describe our ministry journey as a clergy couple, as well as reflect on some contributions this ministry style can make and is making in the church as a whole. First, our story.

As a couple, we have experienced a variety of ministry settings. We began with Paul serving a parish and Norene working as a part-time student who was also involved in traditional pastor's wife roles within the parish Paul served. Then, we each served separate parishes in adjoining communities. Following that, Norene was a full-time student again while Paul served as a hospital chaplain. We are currently both serving on the same staff of one parish.

In this setting, the nature of the positions has been somewhat fluid, in that we began with two three-quarter time calls, increased that to two full-time calls, and are now planning for a full-time call for Paul and a half-time call for Norene with the arrival of our first child. We have found that each of these settings calls for flexibility in dealing with the challenges of structuring both work and home life.

We would like to begin by describing life as a clergy couple in the same ministry setting.

Life as a Clergy Couple

Four and a half years ago when we considered the calls to our present parish, we received many warnings from colleagues and friends regarding the potential dangers of mixing a marriage and a work relationship. The main concern they expressed was the fear that work and home would be so intertwined that pressures in one area would severely and directly affect the other. This was our big concern too. What we have discovered so far is that our marriage and working relationship are more interdependent than couples who do not share the same career setting. (Farming families and "Mom and Pop" businesses understand this dynamic well, as they have worked as husband–wife teams and whole family teams for generations.) This reality creates its own special pressures, for instance:

1. *Work-home responsibilities sometimes collide.* When one person is sick, the other not only gains the extra responsibilities of covering for an absent colleague at work, but also assumes added responsibilities for household chores and family care at home. When there are special pressures at work, they come home with us as well.

2. *Fishbowl existence intensified.* The congregation and our colleagues experience the working out of our ministry and marriage at the same time. The "fishbowl" life-style that many parsonage families have experienced in the past is intensified in a clergy couple relationship. We cannot compartmentalize our lives. At a church council meeting we are colleagues as well as husband and wife.

3. *Competition can divide.* There are two sources of competition for us: one is competition between each other, the second is the comparison made between us by congregational members. These kinds of comparisons are a given for any pastoral team. But again, because the marriage and working relationship are interdependent for clergy couples, competition in the workplace means that more is at stake for us.

Some helps we've found for dealing with competition are:

a. *Expect it.* When we've experienced competition between ourselves or at occasional times when we might be compared against one another by parishioners, one needs to acknowledge it to the other in order to diffuse its potentially destructive power.

b. We have come to realize that *ministry requires a multitude of gifts and no one person has all the gifts.* This may seem an obvious conclusion, but it can actually be very freeing to apply the Apostle

Paul's church-as-body metaphor (1 Cor. 12:12-26) to the clergy couple relationship. In a certain situation, one person's gifts may loom large. In another, the other person's may shine.

c. As in any team, *it is important to upbuild and support one's spouse/colleague for her/his gifts.* In fact, it has often been our experience that working together has more often helped us to appreciate the gifts of the other than to view them as a threat.

4. *The risk of trying.* There is a risk in deciding to work together. No couple can be completely assured that the marriage-work relationship will be a healthy, happy one for them. Some couples may prefer not to try it at all. Others have tried it and discovered that it was not for them. This decision certainly does not imply that those who make such choices have troubled marriages. The arrangement simply may not work for some couples. There are many ministry combinations that do not involve team ministry, such as serving different parishes, hospital, nursing home, military or other institutional chaplaincy, counseling, or teaching. As we entered a setting in which we found ourselves working together, we decided together on these priorities:

First, we agreed that the health of our marriage is our highest priority. If we were to see that our working together was somehow hindering our marriage, then we would be prepared to make changes as necessary to restore the health of our marriage.

Second, we found that working out the everyday details of this new relationship was greatly aided by the help of an impartial third party. We were fortunate to have a Lutheran Social Services counselor in our town who listened, observed, and counseled us, especially in the beginning.

Third, we decided to refrain from daily evaluation of our progress or success as a team. The tensions of any new job are great. After a couple of years, we looked at our marriage and work relationship and realized we were enjoying ourselves immensely. With the help of some history from which to draw, we took daily ups and downs less seriously.

5. *Will the real pastor please stand up?*

(Norene): For me, the question often arises: "Do you think of yourself as a pastor or a pastor's wife?" The answer, of course, is that I am both. Because I am both, I may experience a certain mixing of these roles at times. People may say things like, "This is our pastor's wife. She's also a pastor." While that might be interpreted as a discount of my role, I usually choose to believe that it is more a case of vocabulary catching up to a new reality. There are a few people who simply cannot imagine a woman as a pastor. Fortunately, these are rare in comparison to those who have expressed appreciation and support.

Especially in the first year, I was sensitive to any hint that I might not be considered Paul's equal. We found it important to divide evenly and strictly all pastoral responsibilities to help avoid this. It is also good for me when Paul is gone for a week or more of continuing education as the total on-call responsibilities for the congregation are mine. During his first absence in the first year, I had three funerals in two days. After that, my confidence in my ability to "do the job" increased exponentially!

When another person (or I, myself) question the authenticity of my call, I sometimes take out my Letter of Call and review *who* has called me and what I am called to do. I also remember that the Apostle Paul before me had such problems (Gal. 1:1— 2:21) as did Martin Luther. It helps to be in such august company.

The pressure and concerns we have related are real. Sometimes they may become a heavy load. There are also many pluses in working together. It allows us time together while living out our vocations outside the home. And, as another clergy couple put it, "When the moving van pulls into the parking lot, the clergy couple already is operating at a high trust level, with built-in knowledge of each other's strengths and weaknesses." (Judith L. Weidman, ed., *Women Ministers*, Harper and Row [1985], p. 213.)

Sometimes we realize that the content of our relationship is dominated by our work life. But, over the course of the year, we have learned to take some moments in the week and some weeks of the year that are less hectic to be together and refresh our marriage. For us, the opportunity to work with one's spouse as a colleague has far outweighed the hazards of working together.

Sharing the Tasks

Like many other teams, we divide our responsibilities as equally as possible, in the following way: we preach alternate weeks, while the non-preaching colleague has responsibility for the liturgy and hospital visitation. Night hospital and emergency calls are usually covered by the nonpreaching spouse. This allows us a natural one week "on" and one week "off" call. We also alternate officiating at funerals and weddings. We usually cover weddings alone and both participate in funerals where we alternate officiating and assisting roles.

Each of us has primary responsibility for certain council committees, that follow our current interests and expertise. We try to avoid working in each other's fields if at all possible. If one person has an idea or suggestion for the colleague's committee, the suggestion is communicated to the colleague and not directly to the committee so as not to confuse committee members. Paul relates to the junior high youth, while Norene has leadership of the senior high. Either of us may attend events specially held for people younger than seventh grade. We both have generally equal responsibilities for counseling, administration, and visitation, though Paul has perhaps a few more administrative tasks than Norene.

In general, we employ the work divisions used by other teams in which a nonhierarchical, co-pastorate model is followed. This system has worked well for us and we think has worked well for the congregation.

New Visions for the Whole People of God

In his intriguing book, *The Prophetic Imagination*, Walter Brueggemann sets forth this hypothesis: "The task of prophetic ministry is to nurture, nourish, and evoke a consciousness and perception alternative to the consciousness and perception of the dominant culture around us" (Walter Brueggemann, *The Prophetic Imagination*, Fortress [1978], p. 13).

Is it too audacious to believe that the presence of a clergy couple, or a nonmarried male–female clergy team can help to evoke among our people the "alternative consciousness" which Brueggemann attributes to prophetic ministry? Is it possible that women and men who share all aspects of ministry between them constitute an alternative vision in our society? We think so. Especially in Sunday morning worship, where the powerful symbols of the here-and-not-here kingdom of God spark our imagination, we long to envision a new way of being in the world. For much of the world, mutuality between the sexes is one such vision of the Kingdom of God. To the extent that we are able to awaken our people to this alternative consciousness as a clergy couple, we hold a valuable place in the church's ministry.

Often that alternative consciousness is called forth in everyday ways in the life of the parish. Here is one such example:

About a year ago, one of our District Ministers was invited to spend a weekend with us to experience the life and community of our rural Southwest Minnesota District parish. At the end of his visit, while meeting with the church council, he noted a number of areas in which traditional sex role stereotypes had changed. One of the most surprising places of change was the Sunday morning staffing of the nursery. Long the exclusive domain of women and teenage girls, the nursery was now also staffed with teenage boys and occasionally grandfathers. When we discussed how this change had come about, we recalled for him the intentional process by which men had been included in this care-giving ministry. And, while the change had come about in a very intentional way, the surprising thing was noting how readily it had been accepted in a rather conservative and traditional setting. "Perhaps," the District Minister speculated, "this is because of the modeling of the pastoral team which provided a leadership model of mutuality between women and men. This model is helping to break down stereotypical sex roles."

When mutuality is seen as an image of the kingdom of God, then people begin to see ways in which it can be embraced in all areas of congregational life. Through the lens of mutuality, two things become very clear. First, we see the many ways in which men have been systematically excluded from the care-giving/nurturing ministries of the church, such as the care and nurture of children, the bringing and serving of food, Bible study and prayer.

Second, we see the ways in which women have been systematically excluded from positions of leadership and decision making, except within their own separate organization. This sex role stereotyping takes place early on in life and in subtle ways, as we discovered with the nursery staffing.

Now, men are increasingly included in the caregiving, service areas of ministry within our congregation. For example, they are being incorporated into the work groups assigned to serve weddings and funerals. These groups are being further expanded to include whole families. Though this integration is not yet a complete reality, the structures are changing to allow inclusiveness to become a reality. Often, boys were not asked to bring treats to youth group activities. Now they are asked too. Men and women are participating together in Bible study and prayer through programs like Search Weekly Bible Studies.

Women are now being called out for positions of leadership traditionally held only by men, such as council president, members of the property and finance committee, and so forth.

There are probably a number of reasons why these changes have been made and, for the most part, accepted. We believe that the presence of a clergy couple working in mutuality may well have accelerated the change in this community. The modeling of mutuality between the sexes in both work and marriage relationships is one gift that clergy couples can give to God's people, the church.

If the vision of the kingdom of God is one that includes all people, then the leadership of the body of Christ must reflect this rich diversity. Clergy couples are one group among many who help us see how and in what ways we can more fully embrace the world-transforming call of Christ in this age. We need this rich diversity in order to embody more fully the vision of God's kingdom.

Finally, it is important to mention that we are in our present situation because of the strong yet sensitive advocacy of our bishop and synod staff. Though times are changing, it is still vitally important that people in leadership roles in the church maintain their commitment and vigilance in the placement of clergy couples and women. Without this intentional and often courageous advocacy, many gifted and trained people will not receive calls to parishes and other ministry settings.

To our congregation and every congregation who breaks new ground by calling women and clergy couples to serve them—our deep thanks.

"For still the vision awaits its time:
it hastens to the end—it will not lie.
If it seem slow, wait for it;
it will surely come, it will not delay."

(Habakkuk 2:3)

12

The Pastor and the Authority of the Office

RUTH DREWS

My office is a wreck. The ancient threadbare Oriental rug is getting all ripped up from the junior high Sunday school class which meets here. I have a whole wall of book-shelves, built in early July. Now, several months later, they are still empty, of books at least. In fact, the sawdust from their construction is still all over the rug. I have no time to put the books on the shelves, and it's embarrassing also to realize that I have even survived quite well for these months without access to any of these books. It's more embarrassing to realize that I don't even notice any of this until I remember that I have a meeting with someone important, like an insurance person or a couple for marriage counseling or a synod official, and I imagine what they are thinking about my office.

Being a pastor/developer of a new mission congregation in an urban setting, I see my work as taking place largely outside my office, out on the streets and out among people, so the state of the office goes largely unnoticed. But it also suffers from the normal state of affairs. Ministry here in the inner city seems to be a process of bouncing from "crisis to crisis," as my intern supervisor would describe in his German accent. When a bullet grazes the head of a youth group member bicycling down the street, when a family has to move to a welfare hotel in the next town, when the carefully arranged Baptism is about to fall through because the godparents and the parents had a fight, when a chunk of the old ceiling plaster falls on the organ on Friday and damages the major pipes so that they only whistle, there just doesn't seem to be a whole lot of time to put books on book-shelves.

I suppose, however, that it is precisely this "crisis to crisis" nature of urban ministry which excites, energizes, and keeps me at it. I have been blessed to have found my niche in urban ministry, in this setting which nourishes me, in this work which uses the gifts God has given me for ministry. I am grateful for that niche, and I know that many search for a long time to find their own place of fulfillment. Recently passing the six-year anniversary of my ordination, I have been surprised at how often I realize that I really have been doing this for awhile, that I may be specialized, or perhaps too "narrow" in my vision, and that the time actually *does* make a difference in my experience (of course) and confidence (surprise!). I find myself saying things with assurance and then wondering if I really have the authority to say them, and then realizing that I have a reasonable amount of wild, difficult, and wonderful experience under my belt. I have failed and succeeded, struggled and lost and won, and I have kept at it with joy.

It certainly never looked like this from the outside. I grew up in a church with a pastor who had been there 38 years, and a series of vicars, some of whom were interesting but most of whom seemed stuffy, or worse. I do not in fact remember if they wore clerics most of the time or not, but I do remember that every so often my brothers and I played at wearing "pastor shirts" (you put a collared shirt on backwards), so we must have been observing something. However, I can also remember a family discussion of a photo in the newspaper, of cleanup day at the local polluted river (back when ecology was a popular cause). One of the area Lutheran clergy participated, wearing his collar, and I can remember my parents' comments on how ridiculous and stuffy they found that to be.

Attending a nondenominational seminary gave me the opportunity to experience a wide variety of attitudes towards authority
and towards clerical collars. Most of us seminarians were thrilled
by the calling, and awed or terrified by its responsibilities. I think
our ambivalence was reflected by the low esteem in which the
wearing of a collar was held. Only one Episcopal professor could
get away with it, but we all knew he was rather starchy anyway.

I parachuted into a new world on internship, landing in the
middle of a lively multiple-point city parish in a *very* poor, predominantly black and Hispanic city. The question "What is this
white girl doing *here*?" was probably equally strong in my mind
as it was in the minds of the people in the neighborhood! It was
clear to me that wearing a collar gave me a quick and easy identity,
and made my purpose in that neighborhood at least a little bit
clearer. Within four days I went out and bought my first clergy
shirts and wore them.

In that community, it was clear first of all that a title was part
of the authority given by the people to their leaders. I was called
the Vicar, or Vicar Ruth; but there had not been an intern there
for awhile, so people were not quite sure what "vicar" meant. I
also got called "Victor Ruth"! As time went on it seemed that
parents were telling their children, "She is an adult, so you can't
just call her Vicar Ruth," and I became "Miss Vicar Ruth" for
most of my time there. That has been my continued experience
in black communities, so I have at times been called "Miss Pastor
Ruth" in both Chicago and New Haven. I had begun by worrying
terribly that a title or titles would somehow be off-putting to
people. My experience was that either my fears were unfounded,
or my personal demeanor was able to overcome whatever dis-
tancing a title or titles might create.

I believe that inner city ministry necessitates a *great* deal of
contact with people on their turf, of visibility and identity as a
recognizable person in a recognizable role in that neighborhood.
I spend a great deal of time walking the streets, dressed in clerics,
wearing out my shoes. A lot of other people, of course, also spend
a lot of time on the streets. Every two or three months I have
had the experience of walking past a group of people, one of

whom will turn as I pass and ask in disbelief, "You a preacher!?" To which I can smile and reply, "Of course I'm a preacher. Don't I look like one?" And we all laugh, because the answer is obviously yes and no. And the ice is broken for the establishing of another relationship. Actually, my favorite variation of this experience is the time when I passed a group of people, and one said, "Hey baby, nice legs." I turned around and said, "Excuse me?" The man was extremely taken aback and said, "Oh, I'm sorry! I didn't know you was a preacher! I was trying to pick you up." Well, the conversation could have gone in about eight different directions from there. Unfortunately, I did not quite have the presence of mind to reply, "Nice legs? Of course, I am created in God's image!" Nor was there time for the discussion that would have ensued from *that* remark.

All of this is to say that some authority is given, given by the community or parish, and given by the community of the gathered congregation from that parish. Authority and respect, particularly as I have experienced it in black communities where I've served, is (still) given to clergypersons. I "dress like a preacher" because I *am* a preacher. I am not a social worker or police officer or lawyer. The simple matter of dress, in such a community, saves me two or three months of work right from the start.

Yet I also need to be willing to *take* the authority that the communities (both parish and congregation) give me. To say in some way that "I do not really want" or "I do not deserve" the authority that rests upon me in this office is, I believe, to deny the strange and wonderful workings of the Holy Spirit which have called me to this place at this time. We need to struggle with the continued ambivalence that women carry towards authority. We need boldly to take on the authority granted to us, with courage and trust in God's continued help and support.

I know full well that this is easier said than done. Often I am asked about how I am accepted as a woman minister. I answer that my sense is that in the situations I've served, people have an urgent need for ministry, to be loved and cared for, to have attention paid to them, to hear God's word of freedom and empowerment. They are appreciative of the pastor and the care offered, and are not particular if it is a female pastor or a male pastor who offers that ministry. Yet I remember an experience with an Hispanic woman, mother of four, whom I visited and conversed with in Spanish quite regularly. Her younger children were eagerly involved in the church, her junior high son excited about the youth group. Her oldest son (16) had gotten deeply involved in drugs and dealing, and she was feeling powerless and at wit's end about him. We shared pain and frustrations, as well as *arroz y gandules* (rice and pigeon peas), and our mutual struggles with another language. One day she told me that she had become so depressed that she had gone to the local Catholic priest, apologizing for her halting English (he knew almost no Spanish), and had had a long conversation with him, which had helped a great deal. It was clear to me that whatever authority I did have in her eyes, I did not have the "clout" or could not offer the assurance, despite our close relationship, that a male Catholic priest could offer. Perhaps because I was not Catholic, or perhaps because I was female as well, despite having the function of a minister, I did not have the *authority* of a minister in her eyes.

My experiences in dealing with a rather complicated church financial situation helped me in my own painful growth in assuming my authority. I served a church with a rather large endowment, controlled, for the most part, by one older male. About two-thirds of the church's yearly budget came from the endowment, rather than from regular congregational giving. The endowment was poorly invested, yielding little or no return. In addition, the amount of the endowment had never been made public, because "people would stop giving if they knew how much money we have." I was horrified at the lack of faith and trust, as well as the illegality and inefficiency of the situation. I figured that we, pastor and church council, could talk it all over for an hour, reinvest the funds, publicize the church's resources as constitutionally mandated, and get on with the mission of the church. Little did I realize that despite being called, ordained, and installed as pastor, a "young girl" like me was certainly *not* perceived as anyone who knew anything about how to invest money. And *what* did *I* know about how people would react? I hadn't been with these people for 40 years! Constitution not-withstanding, the church council was not about to let me "de-stroy" the church.

As pastor, I had the constitutional authority to see that the finances were properly reported, yet I struggled for several months over doing just that. It was a variation on the "Who, me?!" issue in ministry, and in the Bible: "Why should *I* have to do this?" At one point in a long and tear-filled conversation over this issue with a mentor of mine, he said, "You will at some point feel right and able to report those issues properly, to print it in a newsletter or whatever." That did not stop the flow of tears, but it was very reassuring. Later, in a related incident, I received strong affirmation of my ministry in that place from the office of the bishop. When I returned to the issue of properly reporting the finances, I then realized that there was no longer any ambivalence in my mind about doing what needed to be done. My mentor had been right, because it had taken time, as much as the affirmation of the bishop, in order for me to believe in my own authority on that issue.

A pastor is chosen by a congregation, designated by the work-ing of the Holy Spirit in that community as their pastor. We make a covenant with each other at installation, solemnly and joyfully making mutual promises of help and support. But none of us in that covenant is fully aware of what that means, of what is really going on. The pastor is often called to call us to account— in finances, racism, spiritual growth, whatever—yet when she actually does so, she or the people may well ask, "Who, me?" or "Who, her?" I believe that is because we grow together, pastor and people, in our understanding of authority. It doesn't occur to us that the pastor will have to do *this* as well as *that*.

The everyday implications of our special and holy promises are naturally not clear at the outset. We may in fact be in one of those chicken-and-egg situations. We cannot assume authority that people do not grant us. People do not grant us authority if we do not take ourselves seriously. We feel we need more than faith in God's call, in order to take ourselves seriously. Others have faith that we have been called by God, or they would not have called us. Yet they can call us and not grant us the authority, and then whose ambivalence is worse, theirs or ours?

In my experience, the solution to the dilemma is best illustrated by this example. Having lived in several "very tough neighborhoods," where I have been a clear minority, I am often asked if I am afraid to live there. I reply that I am, of course, very cautious, but that basically I *belong* there. I live there, it is my neighborhood, too, and I have as much of a right to walk the streets as anyone else. After all, a neighborhood is just a collection of normal human beings like me. I am sure that this attitude is projected by my body language, and I have never had any trouble so far. I "step out," as it were, because I *belong* there.

I believe the issue of authority is similar. At some point an ordained woman needs to "step out" in God's grace, to reach the turning point and take the step into a different image or perception of herself. All of the factors I have mentioned, and others, play a part in coming to that point, but of course the point itself is as different as we are. It may come too soon or seemingly too late, depending on the unique person that God has created us to be. But it will come.

In my day-to-day visiting as a pastor/developer, I have had to call on some of the neighborhood drug-dealing outposts. That is not exactly a task I wake up in the morning looking forward to with great joy, but it has to be done. I entered one second-floor apartment to greet a group of 6–10 men, and it was clearly a "den" where a "nice young woman like me" did not belong. I tried to make the best of it by introducing myself as the new pastor, and asked for their names. "Well, I'm Amos, and this is Moses, and Joshua over there, and Luke . . ." I figured they were pulling my leg, but I was determined to hold my own, so I said, "Well, I'm looking for Jesus! Where's Jesus?" The room dissolved in laughter, and I believe I could almost *feel* the respect rising, because, I suppose, I had not been intimidated and had been myself. It turned out that most of the men really *did* have biblical names, a large family of brothers whose mother had been a faithful churchgoer and, I imagine, tried to put her sons on the straight and narrow.

On that particular street I am known as "Sister Ruth" to the residents. Once I heard the beginnings of a whistle from a car, and then someone else said, "Shhhh, she's a *nun*." As I laughingly recounted this story to other friends in the neighborhood, one of them chided me, "You shouldn't let them call you that. You're a pastor, not a nun, and they should understand that and take you seriously." I've thought of that comment often, because I think it speaks of what others give us. They can be in step with, or ahead of the times, recognizing that women's ministry can be done by nuns *or* by pastors, and that we need to take seriously who we are and not hedge the question. (Nevertheless, clarification of my status with a group of drug dealers is not something I have attempted yet.)

Reading some of the stories I've shared, it might seem that the voices of affirmation, the words which have confirmed my own sense of authority, have all come from men. I have mentioned several men here, because they have figured in the crisis points which I have chosen to share. But I think the ongoing growth and continued learning about my own authority, the crucial day-by-day and month-by-month development, has been confirmed and nurtured by my sister pastors, my colleagues and foremothers whom I have sought out and treasure as the ones who keep me sane and strong. I give their affirmation equal or even greater value than the affirmation of my male mentors, because they can speak to my soul also. They are female. They understand in a certain special way the life situation and the difference between men's and women's experience on this issue.

I want to close with a final experience, something which has been shared with me by three people in two different parishes. At one or another point in my ministry, a person has come up to me and said, "You know, I'm not quite sure if it is OK to say this or not, but when I see you in front of the church, you make me think of Jesus. You really remind me of Jesus . . ." and they have gone on to share their hesitancy, and comfort, in thinking this way.

Now, I have never known how to respond, or what to make of this. Is this idolatry that should be discouraged? Is this radical rethinking of the God-image which I should encourage? Is this due to nothing more than the fact that I am tall and have long, brown, wavy hair, and in a white robe thus perhaps resemble the typical "weepy Jesus" pictures that are so familiar?

I like to think that these persons are seeing a gift from God, in which we can all rejoice. The Holy Spirit has called me to this place, through the workings of the organized communities of God's people, and given me the strength, courage, and will to serve here. All of these give me the authority to serve in ministry. Yet the most important gift that these persons have seen, I believe, is the "joy of God's salvation," as we sometimes sing in worship.

It is joy, a profound sense of rightness, which affirms me in this office of pastor, and which is mentioned most by the persons who have shared these impressions with me. It is that joy which is truly a gift from God. And even when the joy seems to be in recession, I know that the psalm continues, "Uphold me with your free Spirit." I know that we will be upheld during the night, as surely as joy comes in the morning.

13
Claiming New Space

CONSTANCE F. PARVEY

A decade ago I moved from the parish ministry as a pastor at University Lutheran Church, Cambridge, Mass. and a chaplain at Harvard and the Massachusetts Institute of Technology (MIT) to an administrative position in the church worldwide, the staff of the World Council of Churches (WCC) in Geneva, Switzerland. This, my second call, was to direct a new WCC study entitled "The Community of Women and Men in the Church." The program was located in the Faith and Order Commission and jointly sponsored by Faith and Order and the subunit on Women in Church and Society. I headed up that program which studied the impact on theology and church life of the new leadership roles of women in church and society. Issues addressed ranged from women in authority, to the nature of authority structures themselves, to interpretation of scripture, to the normative male reference point for theology over the centuries and how this has shaped Christian women's lives and socialization. Since that position was ended by the Faith and Order Commission in 1981, I have been teaching, serving mainly as a visiting lecturer at the Vancouver School of Theology in British Columbia, at Bryn Mawr College, in the Department of Religion at Temple University, and presently as adjunct faculty at the Lutheran Theological Seminary in Philadelphia. This chapter is a reflection on the years when I served as a pastor and university chaplain and it looks at only one area of the complexities of ordained women's reality: claiming space.

My last Sunday as a pastor in Cambridge, Mass. was the second Sunday in Advent, 1977, close to the date of my ordination which had been on the first Sunday in Advent, 1972. I was in the Cambridge ministry as an ordained pastor for five years. It was a time of new and exciting beginnings for women in ministry. I was the first woman to be ordained in the New England Synod, the fifth to be ordained in the Lutheran Church in America and the first woman ever ordained at Harvard University since its founding in 1637. The building in which I was ordained, Memorial Church, is itself not old. It was built after World War I as a tribute to the Harvard men who died in that war. Its magnificent colonial style, with the wide, white Greek columns inside and out, and the high, clear, luminous windows, serves some of the same purposes of a Greek temple. It is a reminder of another era, of a classical tradition of learning and of religion in the United States, and in this case, it is also a tribute to those who paid the highest price for safeguarding peace.

A week later I was installed in the ministry at MIT. I received my call to that ministry at a meeting of the Lutheran Directing Committee at MIT that took place in the Draper Room at MIT. This space, though only one room, is also a memorial, this time to a professor, Dr. Charles S. Draper, who was the inventive genius behind the long-range missile tracking systems that are the basis for all guided missile systems in space today. The walls of the room were covered with framed congratulatory letters and citations from heads of state the world over, including the Soviet Union and China.

The symbolic significance of these two spaces was not lost in my years of ministry. These spaces, where my ministry had its inception, were dedicated, one to the tragedies of war, whose sins nations turn to glory, and the other to the adventures and explorations of space conquest, the indomitable American hope. Though I wanted to resist inclusion in either of these, I realized in some profound way that I too am linked to the sagas of these men of the past and to their dreams of the future—of war and the threat of war, of adventures in space, first the moon and later Mars, first for mining the planetary metals and minerals, and now the playing out of the fantasy of "Star Wars." These grandiose dreams of youth have since become the serious preoccupations and priorities of leading men of our nation.

I am linked to these ventures not because I was the person who decided on them, or voted for them but because this is my country and it is to the Christian community within this country that I am called to minister. Yet, in an equally profound way, the decisions and actions that led to the building of Memorial Church and later to Draper Lab are not part of my priorities or values for our nation and I do not claim them as my own. In college when I was approached to initiate and organize a women's division of the ROTC at the University of Minnesota, I turned the invitation down. It was not out of disloyalty to my country, but out of loyalty to my faith commitments and to a vision of power as a strategy of learned, intelligent diplomacy and vigorous commitment to peace, not to more and more stockpiling and saber rattling. Power has many forms and no civilization has survived long that depended mainly on its military might.

When I was ordained in 1972, though the Viet Nam War was raging, the student uproar of the late '60s was coming to an end. Students had made their statements about the role of defense department contracts in university research and the role of the ROTC. The era when I entered this scene was one when many students, the younger sisters and brothers of the class of '68, were quieter. Yet I found them no less serious about putting together their sense of social responsibility with alternative methods for making peace, and struggling to make sense of this in terms of their own vocational and life-style choices. I saw my ministry as one that probed issues of space, not outer space, but inner space; not returning to individualism and retreating, but building and fostering community contexts where reflection could take place; to experience and find new grounds for approaching human relationships and critical political and social issues.

Among the groups that were founded to work on these issues was the Green Table, drawing mainly older students from the graduate schools at Harvard and MIT. In addition to organizing topical discussions ranging from world hunger to human rights violations and liberation theology, they, both female and male graduate students, also learned to cook for groups of twenty or more using the book, *Diet for a Small Planet* by Frances Moore Lappé. What seemed a bit esoteric at the time has since become a much more integrated part of the American diet, as more people worry about weight, cancer, and heart disease. Also many are more conscious of the uneven distribution of food and purchasing power throughout the world, which leads increasing numbers of people to the edge of starvation or beyond. At MIT as well, students discussed and argued about what they were learning and seeing around them, about the technologies of the future and the ethical, moral issues they raise. Many students, American and international, questioned how they could use their MIT education for peaceful purposes and still have an income that would support a family. Women students were gradually increasing in numbers during this time, and they brought with them their insecurities about making it in a competitive world and their questions about the new worlds of science and technology that they were training for.

In these first years, space and the claiming of space were everywhere around me and other women, especially the MIT women I observed, who were naming and struggling with deeply ingrained male structures, mentalities, and ways of doing things, and trying to sort them out for themselves. Fledgling questions began to be asked about women in science and math and engineering. Might women in charge go about their work differently, have different priorities? Would women think differently about the future because they will be mothers and will have the concrete future of their children in mind? Could women do both: be good professionals and also good mothers? These were questions with unknown answers.

There were questions of space on a mini-level as well. In my pastoral role at University Lutheran Church I started out with my office in the basement, in a dark corner room with a small wired-over window, as far away as one could be from the church office and yet stay in the building. It was actually a dangerous place as well, with no way to get out or call for help should my life be threatened, and churches can be dangerous places. There was more than one attempted robbery right in my office and there were other life-threatening moments. After two years the property committee and the church council were convinced that my office should be moved to the second floor, to take over a room that was used as a nursery for only two hours a week. At last I had two big windows and my office was now much closer to the weekday center of activity; my own part-time secretary had a place to work as well. For me, the church office is the kitchen of the congregation and a pastor, like a good cook, can't function at a distance from it if she/he wants creative results.

Other spaces to be claimed were related to the liturgy, even to the clothes that I wore. There were no albs or cassocks or chasubles for women. Since I was tall, I had to buy one that would have fit a man of about 250 pounds when I was about half that body weight. A marvelous Roman Catholic seamstress in Cambridge (I call her Dorcas) recut the shoulders, sleeves, and neck to fit my body form. I didn't need as much physical body space as most men my height.

Another consideration was the care of liturgical vestments customarily provided by women of the church. When I began my ministry I thought I might have some hassles with the altar guild over washing the liturgical garments of a woman pastor. I could hear the tapes in the minds of some of them, "She's a woman, like us; she can do it herself." In that setting I thought I would be expected to take care of myself, and indeed, I also wanted to. If my presence was going to help free other women for new roles in the church, then I needed to pay attention at the beginning to what my hopes were for myself and for other women, for indeed for the first time in the history of the Lutheran church in that place, I, their pastor, was "like them!" With a woman pastor it would be easier for women to sort out the difference between (1) what women are socialized to do for a man and how that affects the relationship between male clergy and women laity, and (2) what women will do for a woman who is their pastor. It is an occasion for spiritual reflection, personal emergence, and faith development for female persons with an identity we name for ourselves rather than one given to us by men.

Then there was the issue of stoles. I didn't want the cardboard stiff stoles that many clergymen at that time were wearing which stand up whether someone is in them or not. I was lucky as the seasons came around that various friends made sure that I had lovely, soft, but strongly colored and deeply textured, handwoven stoles for all of the liturgical times, all woven by women. This was not planned, but a fact much remembered and appreciated. As women weave the threads of everyday life the world over, they also have done and continue to do much of the spinning, weaving, and embroidery of the vestments appropriate to sacred space and time. As the years have passed and I have attended the ordinations of other women, I have noticed a similar preference for the depth of color and the soft line. I am sure there will be women who will prefer the hard edges. I rejoice in that. We are not all alike. This is one myth which the women's movement has broken.

During the liturgy, when I wore my alb and stoles, I looked like a pastor/priest, but I did not look like a man. This was also true with reference to wearing the clerical collar. Again, the neck sizes were way too big for me and "Dorcas" skillfully tailored them to fit. Though some people urged me to wear black and even black pantsuits (to look like my male colleagues) I chose a black clergy collar, but wore blazers and skirts in browns, grays, and dark blue, in wool and cotton fabrics instead of shiny or synthetic materials. To be "one of them," I did not have to copy male pastors' ways of attire. By virtue of my ordination I was one of them. A rite of the church acting with the help of the Holy Spirit, made me profoundly one of them, not a look-alike.

I am one of them, but I am also profoundly different. I am a woman, with a woman's body and a woman's experience, and my model for ministry is based on my own human foundations and not merely adapted from the style of my male colleagues whose bodies, religious culture, socialization, and life experience is vastly different from mine. Opening up the ordained ministry to women does not mean making us honorary men, merely joining a male club that has opened up its membership card to women if we pass the seminary test and synod examining committees. Having women in the ministry will mean that the ministry which God has in mind for the people of God will be enhanced, that all women, and men with them, will begin to see each other in a new light—and equally important, see ourselves as more developed human beings, pastors, and spiritual guides. I see a change and women in ordained ministry in all the churches are a part of it, as are lay women and sisters in the Roman Catholic and Orthodox churches whose struggle is also ours, but who face structures that are different.

In claiming space liturgically as a woman pastor, I did not understand myself as taking it away from someone else, or merely filling a role where once a man had been. My very presence was saying something different about the relationship between women and men—bodily, sexually, spiritually. What might be hard for women in seminary today to realize is that only 18 years ago, the sacred space was male turf. It was foreign if not "forbidden" territory for women from some traditions. This makes it especially difficult for women today to claim the entire sacred space with the gifts of spiritual authority. Women have been taught that spiritual authority comes from men. Even when we are given this apostolic authority, it is something we learn to claim for ourselves. It is a risk, however, and some are able to take more risks than others.

I have noticed many women presiders who don't stand right in the center of the sacred space; they are a little to the side. With others the voice quivers even when it is strong and trained, or perhaps an ankle is turned, or something about the body is not supported. I have learned how important it is to extend my arms so that they include everyone, and to find the strength in my voice that will fill the space, and to walk around in it as one of the instruments God uses to proclaim to others the promise of "the inheritance with all the saints of light." It is powerful and frightening to be the one in the center through whom these words of the liturgy come. It is awesome; and sometimes with the awe there is also fear or a sense of unworthiness as the prophet Isaiah experienced in the Jerusalem temple, crying out in response to the theophany of God, "Woe is me! For I am lost. . . ." (Isa. 6:5). Though the words of the liturgy have been arranged by humans on the printed page, these words, often the words of Scripture, when spoken in the midst of a praying community, take on a spiritual reality that is far beyond the speakers. Though I seldom do the liturgy at this particular time in my life, I still find myself carried by the words, as I am a carrier. I find that I cannot just sneak into the center and stand there unsure of myself because it is not me but the Holy Spirit that is at work. I have watched women who simply move too fast. They claim the space and run as though they are being pursued on a baseball diamond. During my early days in ministry, I found that I had to practice and practice and practice until I could claim my full bodily and spiritual space at the altar with my full voice and presence.

Since no one like me, of my sex, had occupied this particular space in Christian history, (or if they had, the tradition has been lost), it wasn't easy to learn how to claim it and look natural, as though I had been there since the beginning. What was my pattern to be? Women in ministry today talk about the need for role models; my experience is that they are hard-won. At least for awhile we are on our own, until there is a range of models from which individual women can make choices. My own bias is that we don't settle into role models too quickly. After hundreds of years of not being there, we need time and space and practice to evolve what is ours to contribute for the enhancement and needs of the church now and in the future.

I think back to a time long before I became a pastor. I was raised in North Dakota, in a village called Fredonia, just south of Jamestown. As a child I spent a lot of time on my grandfather's farm, just seven miles away in the open country. One of my favorite places to play was on the hill behind the house. From that hilltop I could see as far as the eye could see, north and south, east and west. There were large boulders on the hill, too huge to remove. One was long and narrow and flat on top. I used to take my miniature English tea set up there and serve tea, either to my twin girl cousins, or sometimes alone to the heavens. I would imagine the oceans far away and the millions of people beyond them. I would serve them tea. There was plenty of space for everyone. There was no need to claim it. It was a gift.

At my ordination service in Memorial Church in 1972, as I was consecrating the elements and lifting them up for all to see, what came into my mind was the picture of serving tea to the people of the world, under the arch of God's gracious creation, on the hillside behind the farm. Last summer I went back to that place. The farm is gone. There is hardly a trace of where it was. The boulders are gone, moved by the heavy machinery of the modern farm, so that the land can be cultivated. But the hill was still there, and the memory still vivid. In God's eyes there is plenty of space for everyone. My wish for all women in ministry, ordained and lay, is that we claim that God-given space which is a gift for the building up of new communities of witness and prayer.

14

Ecumenical Conversations: An Absent Presence

CAROL J. BIRKLAND

In 1986, with the assistance of a fellowship grant, I received a year of ecumenical education in Geneva, Switzerland. Adjacent to the Ecumenical Center which houses the offices of the World Council of Churches, the Lutheran World Federation, and a number of other ecumenical agencies, is the World Council Library. On its walls one can observe the history of women's participation in the ecumenical movement.

There is a historic photograph of the International Missionary Conference held at the Château de Crans in 1920. Thirty-nine serious looking men join five equally serious looking women as they sit for the meeting's formal portrait. Nobody is smiling. In calling for a "world league of churches," did they have some premonition of what lay ahead?

In a way, the history of the World Council is told via its periodic assemblies. One observes, in the photographs lining the library's walls, the increasing number of women's faces appearing at these assemblies and other important meetings. Soon women begin to take their places in the first two rows rather than consistently in the back three.

Today, women are much in evidence in the corridors of the World Council. Granted, many of them are office support staff, but they are executives as well. There have been women Associate General Secretaries and today an American Lutheran woman, Ruth Sovik, serves as moderator of Unit II. This portfolio encompasses the areas of justice and service. With a few exceptions, women are well represented in the World Council's life and work units.

The Commission on Faith and Order is another matter. Charged with the responsibility of encouraging doctrinal convergence from the ranks of a divided Christian world, Faith and Order continues to this day to be dominated by a staff that is largely male, ordained, and academic. It is also important to note that the Roman Catholic Church, while not a member of the World Council of Churches, does participate in the activities of the Faith and Order Commission.

Why should women, both clergy and lay, be concerned about this lack of representation? The main reason, I think, has to do with the issue of ministry. Women clergy, as well as laypeople, both women and men, should be concerned when they read documents which, for the sake of ecumenical convergence, encourage a type of ministry that is both hierarchical and exclusive in nature.

The Baptism, Eucharist, and Ministry Document

Let us take a look at the Faith and Order document, *Baptism, Eucharist, and Ministry,* known in ecumenical parlance as *BEM. BEM* was unanimously adopted at Lima, Peru, in 1982 and represents years of tireless work on the part of many distinguished, committed theologians. Now the document is being circulated to member churches of the World Council for their discussion and reception. It is not a binding document in that it will, on its own, make ecumenical convergence happen. It will, however, serve as a basis for succeeding doctrinal discussions. Therefore, since it will become an ecumenical "building block," undoubtedly gaining acceptance as a major ecumenical reference point, it is important that laity and clergy—especially women clergy—know what decisions have been made by their ecumenical representatives, decisions that they are now being asked to support.

Fully recognizing the positive aspects of much of what *BEM* says, as a laywoman I am troubled by the statement on ministry because of its almost total preoccupation with ordained ministry. After an initial six paragraphs dealing with the calling of "the whole of humanity to become God's people . . . to discover, with the help of the community, the gifts they have received and to use them for the building up of the Church," the next 49 paragraphs are exclusively devoted to a discussion of the ordained ministry and how it is to be ordered. It is as if lay ministries either did not exist, or were not deemed important enough to be discussed. I suspect it is a combination of the two. (All references to the *BEM* document are found in *Baptism, Eucharist and Ministry*, World Council of Churches, Geneva, 1982).

Equally troubling is *BEM*'s narrow vision of the forms the ordained ministry should take. In order for ministry to be valid, and thus recognized by the Roman Catholic Church, it must be threefold in nature; that is, bishop, presbyter, and deacon, and its authority is to be solely based upon apostolic succession.

At this point something must be said about the validity of doctrinal diversity and how such diversity is compatible with ecumenical convergence. Ecumenism does not mean herding all of divided Christendom into one, indistinguishable superchurch. Neither should ecumenism force any church or group of churches to adopt traditions and styles of ministry that have become, as George Lindbeck says, "accidentally necessary" because of historical circumstance (George A. Lindbeck, *The Nature of Doctrine: Religion and Theology in a Postliberal Age*, Westminster [1984], p. 86).

From the very beginning of the conversation, the words "ecumenism" and "reform" have been used together. When one enters into dialog, there is the risk that one's ideas might be changed. Ecumenical convergence has always meant that all parties in the dialog would, in one way or another, be reformed and transformed. Therefore convergence is not to be achieved at the expense of capitulation, but through a process of mutual reform.

However, a number of theologians, Protestant and Roman Catholic alike, have noted that *BEM* tends to encourage more doctrinal adjustment from the churches of the Reformation than it does from Rome.

Unfortunately, *BEM*'s statement on ministry, while correctly stating that the New Testament does not describe any one form of ministry as being valid, nonetheless encourages some churches to "recover the sign of the episcopal succession," even though "episcopal succession (is) a sign, though not a guarantee, of the continuity and unity of the Church."

Deciding to "recover" apostolic succession means that Lutherans would agree with Roman Catholic doctrine that deems Lutheran ministry "defective" since there were no bishops willing to ordain Lutheran clergy after the Reformation. Apostolic succession was broken and as a result Lutheran ministry lacks the "fullness" that is found in the Roman Church. Therefore, it is impossible for Lutherans and Roman Catholics to share the Eucharist. According to Vatican II's *Decree on Ecumenism*, the churches of the Reformation have not "preserved the genuine and total reality of the eucharistic mystery" (Unitatis redintegratio, no. 22 in W.M. Abbot, ed., *The Documents of Vatican II*, America Press [1966], p. 364).

However, Roman Catholic theologians like Avery Dulles have questioned the validity of apostolic succession itself. Dulles says that since the episcopal office did not become universal until the second or third century, the claim to an unbroken line of succession is historically weak. "The view that the Bishops of the Catholic Church have orders stemming without interruption from the Twelve probably cannot be disproved," he says, "but it seems highly improbable in the light of available historical evidence" (Avery Dulles, S.J., "Succession apostolorum-Successio prophetarum-Succession doctorum," *Concilium*, 148 [8/1981]: 65).

The churches of the Reformation have always maintained that apostolic succession is more closely associated with faithfully preaching the gospel and administering the sacraments than with an unbroken line of authority.

Apostolic succession and the orders of bishop, presbyter, and deacon go hand in hand. Again *BEM* states that the New Testament testifies to "a variety of forms which existed at different places and times," but that in the second and third centuries, "a threefold pattern of bishop, presbyter, and deacon became established as the pattern of ordained ministry throughout the Church."

One does not disagree that the threefold ministry became "an established pattern"; but that should not mean it is to be the *only* pattern throughout the church.

In all communities, authority is necessary to avoid anarchy. Division of labor is also a more or less universally accepted tool for bringing order to chaos. However, the question here is not the need for exercising authority in the church, it is rather the concern about how sinful people have abused and continue to abuse power, especially the kind of power that supposedly comes from God and is interpreted for the church-at-large by an elite few.

It is interesting that the advocates of the threefold pattern of ministry plead their case on the basis of historical arguments, when it is history itself that makes the churches of the Reformation so justifiably nervous.

Edward Schillebeeckx says that there is a twofold historical lesson to be learned about the institutionalization of church authority. First, one should always keep in mind the tension between charisma and its institutionalization, because ministry without charisma becomes starved, and can turn the church into nothing more than a power institution. On the other hand, charisma without any institutionalization can breed a community of fanatics who judge everything subjectively and thus risk becoming the "plaything of opposing forces" (Edward Schillebeeckx, *Ministry, Leadership in the Community of Jesus Christ*, Crossroad [1981], p. 24).

In order to hold charisma and institutionalization in creative tension, Leonardo Boff suggests that the church be both an *ecclesia docens* and an *ecclesia dicens*. However, he says, the *dicens* (church, hearer of the Word) should at times have precedence above the *docens* (church, witness to saving events). The church must be both teacher and learner because of the hierarchy's temptation to justify itself.

There is a mutual apprenticeship in the Church: there is a moment when the hierarchy should listen, study the Scriptures, pay attention to the signs of the times. . . there is a moment when lay people must speak and witness to the truth of the gospel applied to the social situation in which they live . . . In those moments the hierarchy feel themselves members of the learning Church, and lay people feel themselves members of the teaching Church. Each is master and pupil of the other and all are followers of the gospel. This coexistence and simultaneity of two functions should bring us to heed Jesus' appeal for no one to be called master, father or spiritual director, since we are all brothers and sisters of one another (Matt. 23:8-10) (Leonardo Boff, "Is the distinction between Ecclesia docens and Ecclesia dicens justified?," *Concilium*, 148 [8/1981]: 48).

Boff warns that any healthy organism can, historically, have its "pathological aspects" which may develop when the church sets up a body of "experts" set apart from the community and thereby expropriates religious power from those who then become "merely lay people." When this happens the church is ripe for a statement like that made by Pope Gregory XVI: "No one can doubt that the Church is an unequal society, in which God has destined some to rule and some to serve. That latter is the laity and the former the clergy" (Ibid., p. 50).

Pope Pius X was even more explicit: "Only the college of pastors has the right and the authority to direct and govern. The masses have no rights at all except to let themselves be governed like the obedient flock following its shepherd" (Ibid.).

It should be remembered that these statements were not made in the Middle Ages, but only within the last 150 years. "All power must know its own limits," warns Boff, "otherwise it falls into the temptation of all power groups, which is to absolutise themselves" (Ibid.).

Frankly, I am amazed and disappointed when I see ordained women supporting the movement to push Reformation churches toward adopting both apostolic succession and the threefold ministry. It is as if they are not quite sure of their legitimacy as clergypersons, and must "buy into" narrow, hierarchical traditions in order to lend more authority to their ministry.

This attitude is shortsighted because in accepting the trappings of traditional church authority, ordained women are treading on slippery ground. Thinking that tradition may somehow "legitimize" their ministries, they fail to see that the same tradition is, to say the least, ambivalent about their claim to be ordained clergy.

If there is one subterranean thread that runs just beneath the surface of *BEM*'s statement on ministry, it is the great hesitancy to come to grips with the issue of women's ordination. One gets the impression that the issue is so ecumenically threatening that in the end it is better to ignore it in the hopes that it will just go away.

Citing Galatians 3 ". . . in Christ there is neither. . . male nor female. . . ," *BEM* generally urges men and women to "discover together their contributions to the service of Christ in the Church. The Church must discover the ministry which can be provided by women as well as that which can be provided by men." *BEM* also meekly says:

> Though they agree on this need, the churches draw different conclusions as to the admission of women to the ordained ministry. An increasing number of churches have decided that there is no biblical or theological reason against ordaining women, and many of them have subsequently proceeded to do so. Yet many churches hold that the tradition of the church in this regard must not be changed.

Is this Faith and Order's idea of breaking new ground on the issue? It is interesting to note that later on *BEM* states:

> Churches which refuse to consider candidates for ordained ministry on the ground of handicap or because they belong, for example,

to one particular race or sociological group should reevaluate their practices. This reevaluation is particularly important today in view of the multitude of experiments in new forms of ministry with which the churches are approaching the modern world.

One may infer then that *BEM* believes that churches who fail to ordain people because of physical handicaps or race should be challenged to reevaluate their policies. However, those who refuse to ordain on the basis of gender, need not be challenged.

Nine Presbyterian feminist theologians responding to *BEM* have reacted to this anomaly by expressing the pain and anger women feel when they "find themselves placed in a position which holds their legitimation as ordained ministers to be of less consequence than that of any other group within the community of faith" ("Feminist Symposium on Baptism, Eucharist and Ministry," *Ecumenical Trends*, November 1984, p. 158).

One wonders how *BEM*'s statement on ministry might have been changed if more women, as well as laymen, had been involved in the deliberations that led to its final drafting. A significant problem for ecumenical conversations is just this: as long as the academic theologians continue to exclude women and laypeople from the arena of theological dialog, we should not be surprised by the results. For far too long, lay people, especially, have been told that since they are not "theologically trained," they cannot grasp the "nuances" of the complex doctrinal issues discussed at the highest levels. What is shameful is not that the academic theologians have said it, but that the laity have believed it.

In February 1987, an international ecumenical conference, organized by the Department of Studies of the Lutheran Council in the USA, took place in Puerto Rico. Of 80 participants, there was one official clergywoman participant. News reports of the conference mentioned that the lack of official women participants was criticized, and one participant even went so far as to say that perhaps the inclusion of laity and parish pastors might have added a "fresh outlook" in addition to that of the regular "ecumenical jet setters."

An Experience of Unity

What I have written might be interpreted as anti-ecumenical; but nothing would be further from the truth. My year in Geneva was, if anything, a time of ecumenical conversion. For five months I was blessed to study, eat, live, (and yes) fight with 48 Protestant, Orthodox and Catholic students from 36 countries in Asia, Africa, Latin America, Europe, and North America.

The Graduate School of Ecumenical Studies at Château de Bossey was the brilliant idea of W. A. Visser't Hooft, the WCC's first General Secretary. Visser't Hooft was an important leader in the ecumenical movement who knew that the essence of ecumenism is that Christians really want to discover the unity we have in Christ. What compels this convergence, in spite of great cultural and doctrinal differences is, fundamentally, a mystery, a mystery I experienced when I lived day to day with Christians of other confessions and cultures.

We intrepid ecumenical students gathered at the graduate school to study the theme of "Gospel and Culture" for five months. To what extent is the gospel the reflection of first century, Hellenistic, paternalistic culture? What manifestations of all cultures fall under the judgment of the gospel? How can culture be used to communicate the gospel? These were the weighty questions before us.

We never answered them. Instead we entered into an ecumenical experience that was not so much theological as it was relational, and it was there that we experienced the Holy Spirit's power—the Spirit's mysterious power—to reconcile us in spite of ourselves.

I'm always amazed when people say, "Well, you know, people are all basically alike." True, we are alike because we are all human beings fashioned by the hand of God; but that is where the "sameness" ends. One thing that my experience at the graduate school taught me is the overwhelming role that culture plays in making us distinctively different, in the way we think and act.

In the beginning we were all so delighted to be together. We were so polite with each other; but soon the novelty of the situation began to wear off and we began to grate on each other.

It was then that the lyrics of a popular song from the '60s came to mind:

The whole world is festering with unhappy souls, the French hate the Germans, the Germans hate the Poles. Italians hate Yugoslavs; South Africans hate the Dutch. And I don't like anybody very much.

It got to the point where national groups were not talking to other national groups. We wondered where the ecumenical spirit had gone. In mid-February the community hit bottom and one entire day had to be set aside to clear the air. We all gathered in the lecture hall and really let each other have it. All of the pent-up animosities came out, and I was sure that a few students, if not more, would simply pack their bags and leave. I personally knew that my life would be no less rich if I never saw some of those people again.

But nobody left. In other settings I am convinced that people would have simply walked away. We, however, could not. In the end words failed us; talking only made things worse. What we needed was to worship together.

We went to the chapel and there I learned the most basic lesson of ecumenism: the Holy Spirit makes of us what we cannot make of ourselves—the reconciled body of Christ.

We celebrated the Lord's Supper, and nobody—Presbyterian, Lutheran, Baptist, Anglican, Roman Catholic, Reformed—questioned the "validity" or "defectiveness" of the celebrant's ministry. Nobody asked, before sharing our Lord's body and blood, if the hand that gave it to us had been given authority to do so through apostolic succession. As God's grace was given to us in the Eucharist, God's Spirit brought healing.

True, the Orthodox did not join us and neither did the Kimbangists of Zaire. Instead, sadly, they reminded us that reconciliation in this world will always be incomplete because the kingdom is here and not yet here. They were an absent presence in our midst.

Separation is a sickness in the Christian church that hinders unity. As an ecumenical group of students we knew the pain of separation. But together, in Communion, we experienced God's grace and healing as the Holy Spirit is literally "turned loose" upon us in the sacrament.

We Need Each Other

In summary, I do not mean to strike out at academics or theologians in this essay. I only wish to point out that all members of the church, clergy and laity, men and women, must be involved in every facet of the ecumenical movement, and that includes the work of the Faith and Order Commission as well.

We must together move toward unity; but that unity must, I think, reflect Jesus' admonition to this apostles in Matthew 20, "You know that among the pagans the rulers lord it over them, and their great men make their authority felt. This is not to happen among you. No; anyone who wants to be great among you must be your servant, and anyone who wants to be great among you must be your slave, just as the Son of Man came not to be served but to serve, and to give his life as a ransom for many."

St. Paul reminds us there are many parts of the body of Christ and each part has a different function. However, every part of the body is dependent on every other part. There is a distinction between parts, but that distinction *never* indicates any kind of hierarchical order. There are a variety of gifts, but no hierarchy of gifts.

Ultimately, we need each other. No group of Christians should be absent from ecumenical conversation. Laypeople need clergy, and clergy need laypeople. In his greeting to the Graduate School students, Emilio Castro, the General Secretary of the World Council of Churches said, "The difficult work involved in ecumenical dialogue is without a doubt important. However, I keep warning the theologians that if they tarry, the laypeople will pass them by."

Parish pastors and laypeople need the academic theologians who comprise the Faith and Order dialogs because while the first lesson of ecumenism is that it is a mystery, the second is that one must know one's own confessional identity before one can be ecumenical. Teaching authority is required; but it must be an authority that recognizes there is always more to be learned and that just maybe some of what we have faithfully learned should be unlearned, or if not, at least ignored.

The academic theologians also need the laity. They need the laity to remind them that sometimes it is necessary to put academic credentials and dedication to doctrinal purity in one's back pocket and let the Holy Spirit be in control. For it is the Spirit that brings unity to the church, the unity for which Jesus prayed.

Contributors

Gracia Grindal graduated from Augsburg College, received a Master of Fine Arts degree from the University of Arkansas, a Masters Degree from Luther Northwestern Theological Seminary, and an LL. D. from Christ Seminary-Seminex. She is the author of two poetry collections, *Pulpit Rock,* and *Sketches Against the Dark* and former editor of *Wellwoman,* newsletter of the Lutheran Women's Caucus. She taught English at Luther College, 1968–1984, and is currently a member of the faculty of Luther Northwestern Seminary. She was recently elected to the Standing Committee of the Office of Ecumenical Affairs of the Evangelical Lutheran Church in America (ELCA).

L. DeAne Lagerquist received her training at California Lutheran College, Luther Northwestern Theological Seminary and the Divinity School of the University of Chicago. Her doctoral dissertation, "That It May Be Done Also Among Us," is a study of Norwegian-American Lutheran women before 1920. She is the author of *From Our Mothers' Arms: A History of Women in the American Lutheran Church.* She served as a member of the planning committee for Women of the Evangelical Lutheran Church in America (WELCA) and as Executive Secretary of the Lutheran Women's Caucus. Formerly Assistant Professor of Theology at Valparaiso University, she is Assistant Professor of Religion at St. Olaf College.

Mary Hull Mohr attended Augustana College, the University of Minnesota, and the University of Colorado where she earned a

Doctor's degree in Renaissance literature. She has taught English at Luther College since 1964. She has served on several committees in the American Lutheran Church (ALC), most recently as the chair of the Standing Committee for the Office of Church in Society. She is a member of the Board of the Commission for Church in Society of the Evangelical Lutheran Church in America.

Anne Kanten is Assistant Commissioner of Agriculture for the State of Minnesota. She is a graduate of St. Olaf College and a former teacher. Anne is one of the women who formed the American Agriculture Movement in the state of Minnesota which organized the farmers' "tractorcade" to Washington, D.C. in 1979. She was a founder of the Theology of Land Task Force of the American Lutheran Church and is a member of the Board of the Division for Global Mission of the Evangelical Lutheran Church in America.

E. Louise Williams is a graduate in theology from Valparaiso University. Following her consecration into the diaconate in 1967, she served in parishes in Kansas City, Mo. and Edmonton, Alberta, Canada. Presently Executive Director of the Lutheran Deaconess Association, Valparaiso, Ind., she is also a part-time instructor in theology at Valparaiso University. She is currently doing work in Christian spirituality in the Graduate Religious Studies program at Mundelein College, Chicago. With Phyllis Kersten she authored *Talented, Tired, Beautiful Feet*, a Bible study for women.

Marlene Wilson is recognized as one of the foremost authorities in volunteer/staff management. Drawing on a wide range of experience in human resource management, she has organized and managed a comprehensive volunteer program which was chosen as a national model. In 1975, she founded Volunteer Management Associates, Boulder, Colo., and has since conducted workshops and conferences for organizations and churches in the United

States, Canada, and Germany. She is the author of three books: *The Effective Management of Volunteer Programs, Survival Skills for Managers,* and *How to Mobilize Church Volunteers.* Ms. Wilson is the chairperson of the Board of the Division for Ministry of the Evangelical Lutheran Church in America.

Eva Rogness served on the Standing Committee on Inter-Church Relations for the American Lutheran Church. She wrote two studies for church youth, *Shouts and Whispers* and *Rejoice, Now We Are One.* She is presently staff chaplain at Abbott Northwestern Hospital, Minneapolis, Minn., on the oncology, hospice, and medical intensive care units.

Janet Landwehr, ordained in 1985 by the Lutheran Church in America, is presently serving Grace Lutheran Church in Freehold, N.J. Her undergraduate degree, from the Massachusetts Institute of Technology, and graduate degree, from Carnegie-Mellon University, are in the field of management, and she worked for some years in business. She took her seminary training at Andover Newton Theological School in the Boston area and Lutheran Theological Seminary in Philadelphia. While a board member of the Lutheran Women's Caucus, she organized its Boston chapter.

Jane Strohl was born and raised in Annapolis, Maryland and received degrees from Vassar College and the Lutheran Theological Seminary at Gettysburg. She was ordained by the Lutheran Church in America and served as pastor of St. John Lutheran Church in Brooklyn, Conn. She is currently a Ph.D. candidate in History of Christianity at the Divinity School of the University of Chicago, with a specialization in Reformation church history and theology. Since autumn 1985, she has served as assistant professor of church history at Luther Northwestern Theological Seminary in St. Paul, Minn.

Stephanie Frey graduated from Luther College in 1974 with a degree in English. After working in the Education Resources

Department of Augsburg Publishing House, she began her studies at Luther Northwestern Theological Seminary where she received the M.Div. degree. After ordination in the American Lutheran Church, she served Christ the King Lutheran Church in
Mankato, Minn. She is presently co-pastor of First Lutheran
Church, St. James, Minn. Her versification of the Magnificat
appears in *Lutheran Book of Worship* (*LBW* 180).

Norene Smith and **Paul Overvold** are a husband–wife team who
serve as co-pastors of Christ Lutheran Church, Slayton, Minn.
They are both graduates of Pacific Lutheran University and Luther Northwestern Theological Seminary.

Ruth Drews earned degrees from Luther College and Yale Divinity School and was ordained by the Lutheran Church in America. After five years in urban ministry at St. Paul's Lutheran
Church in Chicago, and Spanish language training in Puerto Rico,
she is presently pastor/developer of Resurrection Lutheran
Church, a new congregation in "the Hill," a black and Hispanic
neighborhood in New Haven, Conn.

Constance F. Parvey was one of the first women to be ordained
by the Lutheran Church in America. She is a graduate of Harvard
Divinity School, the author of over a hundred articles and three
books, *Come Lord Jesus, Come Quickly; Ordination of Women in
Ecumenical Perspective;* and *The Community of Women and Men
in the Church*. Dr. Parvey directed the Community of Women
and Men in the Church Study for the World Council of Churches
and was a member of the Inter-Lutheran Commission on Worship. She has written the Appendix, "Stir in the Ecumenical
Movement: The Ordination of Women" to Brita Stendahl's book,
The Force of Tradition, A Case Study of Women Priests in Sweden.
She is a member of the Standing Committee of the Office of
Ecumenical Affairs of the Evangelical Lutheran Church in America.

Carol J. Birkland is area secretary for the Middle East and East
Africa with the Division for Global Mission in the Evangelical

Lutheran Church in America. She spent 1985–1986 in Geneva, Switzerland studying at the Graduate School of Ecumenical Studies and interning at the World Council of Churches' Unit II. She earned a Master's Degree in Systematic Theology at Luther Northwestern Seminary. She is the author of *Unified in Hope: Arabs and Jews Talk about Peace.*

Marilyn Preus has had a variety of experience in the church, as musician, teacher, retreat leader, speaker, and writer. She earned a Master's Degree in New Testament at Luther Northwestern Theological Seminary where she is presently teaching a class, "Women in Ministry." She has written several Bible studies, including *Take A New Look, The Role of Women and Men in the World Today; The Gift of Christian Relationships;* and *Blessed for the Journey, A Study of Prayer.*